BEYOND FEAR

Stephanie Slater now lives and works on the Isle of Wight, and is continuing to rebuild her life.

Pat Lancaster is the co-author, with Daphne Parish, of *Prisoner of Baghdad*. She is a journalist with a special interest in women's issues.

BEYOND FEAR

My Will to Survive

STEPHANIE SLATER

with Pat Lancaster

FOURTH ESTATE • *London*

This paperback edition first published 1995
First published in Great Britain in 1995 by
Fourth Estate Limited
6 Salem Road
London W2 4BU

A catalogue record for this book is available from the British Library.

ISBN 1–85702–370–6

'American Pie', p. 32, © 1971, 1972
Mayday Music/Benny Bird Music/MCA Music Publishing,
reproduced by kind permission of MCA Music Limited.

Typeset by Rowland Phototypesetting Limited,
Bury St Edmunds, Suffolk

Printed in Great Britain by ... ... Berks

This book is dedicated to the memory of Julie Dart

Acknowledgements

My sincere thanks to WDC Dee Rhodes, DS Michael Williams, ACC Philip Thomas, WDC Donna Cooper and the many other police officers who helped secure my release and supported me after it. I would also like to thank Danielle Paxton, Lisa Ayscough and my other friends in Great Barr, and Keith Wilkinson, a Birmingham-based journalist assigned to cover my story. The people I have met since moving to the Isle of Wight deserve a special mention for making me feel so welcome, among them my colleagues from Carisbrooke Castle and PC Nigel Parker. I made several new friends during the writing of this book, including my agent Faith Evans, whose advice and encouragement have been invaluable, and Pat Lancaster, the most sympathetic and entertaining co-author anyone could hope for. I would like to thank all the staff at my publishers, Fourth Estate, especially Jane Carr and Joanna Prior. My thanks also to Kevin Watts, to whom I owe my life, and to my Mum and Dad, Betty and Warren Slater, who have been there for me every step of the way. And a final huge thankyou to Stacey Kettner, who has been a never-ending source of humour and emotional support.

Stephanie Slater

I am grateful to a large number of people who have provided me with their expert opinions on matters of law, criminal behaviour and the causes and effects of rape on both attacker and victim, particularly Helena Kennedy and Cheryll Perkins. Thanks also to my colleagues at *The Middle East* magazine, and to Dorothy Alderson for her hospitality during my many visits to the Isle of Wight. Finally, thanks to my family for their support and understanding – especially my daughter Annabelle, who became almost as involved in the project as I have been.

Pat Lancaster

Foreword

by Pat Lancaster

Stephanie Slater became a national celebrity when, in February 1992, she was released from captivity following payment of a £175,000 kidnap ransom. Although abduction is becoming increasingly common – every day children and women are snatched from the security of their homes – kidnap is an unusual offence in the UK. In the annals of contemporary British crime there are no previous examples of the successful handover of a live hostage for a cash ransom.

The story of the twenty-five-year-old estate agent, kidnapped while showing a prospective client around a house in Birmingham and held blindfold in a converted wheely bin for eight days, dominated the headlines of newspaper and television reports. Months later, when her kidnapper Michael Sams was brought to trial at Nottingham Crown Court and given four life sentences for her kidnap, the kidnap and murder of Leeds teenager Julie Dart and a number of attempts to blackmail British Rail, Stephanie was widely praised for the bravery she showed during her captivity. Justice Igor Judge described her survival as being 'entirely due to her own remarkable courage and qualities of character'.

From the minute the police began to work on the Stephanie Slater case they were linking it with the abduction and murder of Julie Dart six months earlier. There were too many similarities to be ignored, and given what had happened to Julie, their hopes for Stephanie's safe return diminished as the days passed. Why did she survive? Her kidnapper, Michael Sams, later admitted to having brutally bludgeoned Julie Dart before strangling her to death. A man capable of killing one woman in cold blood was, the police reasonably assumed, more than capable of carrying out a second murder. But instead of murdering Stephanie, after collecting the ransom money Sams helped her change into clothes he had personally washed and pressed, put her in his car and drove her through dense fog in the early hours of the morning to drop her within a couple of hundred yards of her own front door, to prevent any harm coming to her. At his trial, the prosecution alleged that he had fallen in love with her. Perhaps he had. Certainly a special rapport had developed between them.

As soon as Stephanie had realised she could not physically overpower her attacker, in the house at Turnberry Road, she decided to play along with him. She recalled a book by Dr Miriam Stoppard that she had read years before. The book advised that in the event of a threatened attack it was important to stay calm and remind the aggressor that you are human. Without knowing how long she would have to keep it up, Stephanie decided she would do just that – remain calm and cooperative, and try to establish some sort of relationship with her kidnapper that would help remind him she was a human being with a family and a life. This, she hoped, would make it difficult for him to harm her. That decision probably saved her life.

On her first night in captivity, while she was blindfolded

and handcuffed, Michael Sams raped her. Throughout the period of her release, his capture and right through the trial Stephanie concealed this fact, lying to her parents and the police. The truth would probably never have been told had Sams not boasted to the police, from his prison cell, about a 'special secret' he shared with Stephanie and his later 'confession' to a writer that the two of them had enjoyed a passionate affair during the eight days he held her prisoner in a converted wheely bin in his cluttered workshop.

I discussed Michael Sams' claims and the subject of rape with Stephanie at our second meeting when, in tears, she admitted that it had happened once, on her first night as a prisoner. She might have continued to keep the secret. Sams is unlikely ever to be released from prison and few people take anything he says seriously. However, she felt that if the story of her kidnap was to be told it should be by her rather than by him, and if it was to be told at all, it should be complete.

At the time of her release she was, she says, incapable of admitting she had been raped. After having spent eight days sleeping fully clothed and without a bath or shower, she was already embarrassed by the police examination when she returned home and felt unable to bear the thought of anything more intimate. 'I knew I smelled,' she says apologetically. Her parents, particularly her mother, drew great consolation from believing there had been no sexual contact. 'At least he didn't touch you,' was a phrase Stephanie was to hear repeatedly over the weeks and months following her release. The thought of standing up in a crowded courtroom and speaking in intimate detail of the humiliation she had suffered was more than she could contemplate. 'I knew that to be strong enough to handle the trial in a reasonably composed way, to relive the experience without breaking down, I had to continue with the lie. I am not a liar by nature. To deny there had been sexual contact between us while standing in the witness box and on oath was one of the most difficult things I have ever had to do. It went against everything I believe in but I just didn't have the strength to tell the truth. I didn't want to have to talk about it, I didn't even want to think about it and, I must confess, I didn't want anyone, not anyone, to know that the puny little old man in the dock had been anywhere near me.'

There was, I believe, another fear that Stephanie did not want to confront: the possibility that what she had endured would not be described as rape. She had not, after all, shouted or screamed when Sams forced her to strip and lie down on the mattress; she had merely done as she was told. She spoke feelingly to me of rape cases she had read about in which attempts were made to discredit the victim in open court, when 'perfectly ordinary women are made out to be tarts'. The prospect of this was unbearable. Stephanie is a modern, intelligent woman who, although no goody-two-shoes, was brought up in a working-class home where qualities such as decency and respectability are held in high regard. Sams' allegations of a love affair incense her: 'There was no love affair; there was a rape,' she can now say, with cold determination. But before the matter came out into the open, and before Stephanie had had an opportunity to discuss events with the police and with counsellors, the fear of being castigated for something over which she had no control was horribly real.

Stephanie was kidnapped and taken against her will to the workshop where the rape took place. She did not want to be there and anything that happened was completely beyond her control. Holding her captive was in itself an act of physical assault: she had no free will to exercise during the eight days she was incarcerated in the workshop, she was a prisoner fighting for her survival and a blindfolded, handcuffed victim of a rapist she could not even see, let alone hope to escape from.

Since the trial, Stephanie has made a valiant attempt to reclaim her life but accepts that she will probably never be wholly successful in doing so. There are still fears, associated with the kidnap, that she is forced to confront almost daily. A striking figure, she is frequently recognised, and during the time I have spent with her this has happened on a number of occasions. Even a quick visit to a Chinese take-away can result in recognition, questions and usually sympathy. She appears to take it very much in her stride, although the sense of living life in a goldfish bowl must occasionally be overwhelming.

Perhaps that is why so little remains of the pre-kidnap Stephanie Slater who lived and worked in Birmingham, enjoyed a large circle of friends and was quite happy to walk home alone, through a deserted playing field, after spending an evening at her local pub. These days she is a much more solitary person, sharing a flat with her friend Stacey Kettner on the Isle of Wight. She still enjoys a laugh and a joke but it is more likely to be at home, with a handful of close friends, than in a pub or restaurant, where she might be spotted and approached. 'I know that the Stephanie Slater of before the kidnap has gone for good,' she says with conviction. 'She was confident, ambitious, courageous even – I am none of those. I also have a completely different set of priorities from her. She liked to look good and had high hopes of earning a lot of money, owning her own flat and a sports car, all of which are fairly low on my list these days.

'Well, that's not quite true,' she adds. 'I would like my own place but it would have to be a house, not a flat, and

I would want it for the space and privacy it would afford me, rather than for the acquisitive pleasure of owning something.'

There are obviously some areas of overlap between the characters Stephanie identifies as her pre-kidnap and post-kidnap selves. Many of the characteristics that made her so popular with friends in Birmingham before the kidnap are still evident. She still has a crazy off-the-wall sense of humour, a quick, dry wit and huge generosity. Loyalty, honesty and friendship are qualities she prizes highly, and she is kind and considerate: when rereading the manuscript of this book she removed a number of passages relating to Julie Dart's murder because she felt 'they will only upset her family again', and she is genuinely concerned about the reaction of Teena Sams, her kidnapper's wife, to these latest revelations: 'She's been through such a lot already.'

She is, however, no plaster saint, and the suggestion made by some people that she has made a fortune from her experience and is now salted away living a life of luxury on the Isle of Wight infuriates her. Of the money she received from television and newspaper contracts, almost a third went in tax and what remained is less than she might have expected to earn from her job at Shipways up to the present date, had the kidnap not taken place. Her rented flat on the Isle of Wight is what might be described as a holiday let, comfortable but far from luxurious.

Moving to the island has, she feels, given her an opportunity to recover and grow after the trauma of the kidnap and the trial. Taking a job at Carisbrooke Castle during the summer months, where she was almost constantly on public view, marked a real step forward in this development, and it was not lightly taken. I watched her write at least two letters of resignation before turning up for her first day. 'I don't blame people for being curious. You turn up in their homes day after day in the newspaper or on the television screen and they think they know you; you become public property.

'When I decided to talk openly about the rape I felt very vulnerable all over again. I feel stronger now. I know I can't continue to push it out of my mind for the rest of my life. I have to face up to what happened and deal with it. I should have done it at the time, for all sorts of reasons, but mainly because while I kept silent he still had something over me. When I heard he had said we had a love affair I was furious but, more than that, I was frightened, scared about what my Mum and Dad would say, scared of what the police would say, scared of what people would think of me. I realised that by keeping quiet I was still in his power: even from his prison cell he was still pulling the strings, and I just wasn't prepared to let him do that any more.'

Stephanie feels that if there is any lesson to be learned from her experience it is for women who work, as she did, in vulnerable professions. 'Unfortunately, we don't seem to realise how seriously we put ourselves at risk. In retrospect I feel there are a dozen ways I could have been more protected on the morning I was attacked. If I had had someone else from the office with me, if I had carried a mobile telephone and checked in with the office before entering and again on leaving the property, all of it could have been avoided. Women make up a huge percentage of the workforce – they have a right to be protected – and it isn't just estate agents, it applies to anyone whose job involves meeting up with people outside a normal working environment. Even with the disappearance of Suzy Lamplugh, after the initial horror had passed, nothing much changed. In spite of what happened to me, estate agents are still operating along much the same lines that they always have.

'I sometimes wonder if things would have changed if I had died.'

London
October 1994

·1·

I SHIVERED AS I pulled my dressing gown on, though the bedroom was warm. From the window I could see traces of frost on the lawn below.

'Stephanie!' my mother called up to me for the third or fourth time. 'It's twenty past eight, you're going to be late for work.'

'All right, Mum, I'm up,' I called back, in a voice grumpy with sleep.

I hate getting up, I hate dark mornings and I hate being cold. January is about my least favourite month; there isn't even Christmas to look forward to.

'We're off now, Bab,' my father called from the bottom of the stairs.

He must be dropping Mum off at the shops on his way to work, I thought, as I flopped back on to the bed. Five more minutes . . .

'Yes, all right, see you later.'

'See you later, love, tara.' I heard the front door slam behind them.

I lay completely still. The house was silent except for a barely audible, rhythmical tick that had something to do with the central heating pump. It was only possible to

1

hear it when there wasn't another sound in the house.

I had meant to have a shower and wash my hair before leaving for the office but it was too late for that now. My hair took the best part of half an hour to dry – I would do it when I got home this evening. I thought about what I had on today: a couple of appointments to show people around houses this morning but not much, as far as I could recall, during the afternoon. I wasn't meeting Lisa until seven o'clock so I should have plenty of time for my hair.

As I stared lazily around the room, taking in the familiar posters, soft toys and ornaments, my eyes fell on a brochure on top of the dressing table. Suddenly the events of the previous night came back to me and I was on my feet. Inspired by the holiday adverts on the television I had booked a two-week holiday in July with my friend Danielle on the Isle of Wight. Yesterday confirmation of the booking had come through, and Danni and I had spent the evening planning our holiday. On that bleak January morning July seemed a long time away but the thought cheered me up none the less.

I dashed into the bathroom and as the wash-basin filled with hot water, steaming up the mirror above, I snatched items of clothing out of the wardrobe in my bedroom – underwear, tights, blouse, skirt – and threw them on my bed. I glanced at my watch: it was twenty-five minutes to nine. Strip wash, brush teeth and hair, dress, do make up, feed the cats. I could do it in fifteen minutes and be at work on time if I got a push on.

I turned on the radio, and music accompanied me while I skidded between the open doors of my bedroom and the bathroom, pulling on various items of clothing. As I fastened my blouse I noticed the frost on the lawn again. Rushing back to the bathroom I opened the airing cupboard and pulled out a large white T-shirt of my Dad's,

2

to put on under my blouse. I had been freezing yesterday showing a couple around an empty house in Great Barr. Even the office wasn't overly warm – or maybe it was me: Mum was always complaining that I felt the cold more keenly than anyone she knew.

Buttoning my blouse for the second time I ran down the stairs to find the cats finishing off their breakfast. Great, Mum must have put it out for them before she left. That would save me a couple of minutes. I hopped around, pulling on my boots, as the two cats rubbed against my legs.

'Yes, you're lovely, but I haven't time, I'm late,' I said, stroking their heads.

Just as I was about to leave the house I heard the radio playing upstairs, and hesitated for a moment – should I leave it or not? No, Mum would be back before I was and she would not be happy to open the door and hear pop music blaring through the empty house. I went up and switched it off, intending also to pick up the holiday brochure on the Isle of Wight to take to work.

I had started up the engine of the car before I realised that I had left the brochure lying on the dressing table. Sod it. I hadn't time to go back – I could have another look at it tonight before I went out.

Looking in the office diary, I saw I had a 10.30 appointment at 153 Turnberry Road, just a few minutes' drive away. I'd been there twice before – it was a run-down semi-detached property that had been on the books for some time without attracting much interest. On my first visit I had noticed that the french windows at the back of the house had been broken, probably by kids larking about, since there was no sign of forced entry. And on the second occasion the next-door neighbour came out to tell me that the fence at the back of the property had fallen down. I'd assured her that I would report the damage to the vendor.

During the course of our conversation the woman asked whether I was ever nervous about showing strangers round empty houses. The disappearance of estate agent Suzy Lamplugh some years earlier had increased public awareness of the dangers of the job. Suzy had left her office in London to show a client around a house in the Fulham area and was never seen or heard of again. I was very frightened at the time and for a few months had carried a screecher alarm with me wherever I went, but the memory of the incident faded, and with it the feeling of vulnerability. The alarm was now tucked away in a drawer in the office. I told the woman I didn't allow myself to think about it.

A second glance at the diary, where all appointments and viewings were recorded, told me that my 10.30 appointment was with a Mr Southall, who had arranged the viewing by letter a few days ago. All properties that came into the agency were allocated on a rotation basis to myself or my colleague Jane Cashman: she would take one, and I would take the next. I could just as easily find myself responsible for the sale of a highly desirable detached bungalow that would be on and off the books in a matter of days as for a dump I knew would take months to shift – but then so could Jane. That the sale of 153 Turnberry Road had fallen to me was simply the luck of the draw.

I checked the post and filled the time before leaving to meet Mr Southall by telephoning prospective customers, responding to enquiries and generally sales chasing. My last call took rather longer than I had anticipated and it was already 10.30 by the time I left the office. Fortunately, Turnberry Road was only a few minutes' drive away.

As I parked the car I saw that there was a man standing

in the doorway of no. 153. 'Mr Southall?' I asked. He nodded and muttered 'Yes'. 'Sorry I'm late,' I said, more chirpily than I felt. I liked to be on time for appointments and was annoyed with myself for having kept him waiting. Anxious not to waste any more time I didn't take much notice of the client. During the course of a working week I might see two dozen prospective purchasers and very few made any lasting impact on me. Had things been different, I know I would not have been able to recall Mr Southall in any sort of detail, even a couple of days later.

I had a bit of trouble turning the Yale lock and then I had to push the door hard with my shoulder, because it had jammed. I think I murmured something about the weather, which had been bitterly cold and damp since before Christmas, but he did not respond.

Inside the house it was almost as cold as it was outside. Leaving the front door ajar, as I always did when showing a client round an empty property, I put the door keys on a meter cupboard and walked positively down the hall towards the lounge. Inside the room Mr Southall looked about and made a few cursory enquiries. As he wandered around I took in more of his appearance. He was somewhere between forty and fifty-five years old, with a dark, almost dirty complexion. He was of a medium to stocky build, and quite small, probably only two inches taller than me, which would make him five feet eight inches. His dark hair was brushed back off his face and he wore heavy rimmed glasses, like the ones favoured by Michael Caine. His clothes had a worn look about them and on the breast pocket of his duffle-coat there was a train badge. I didn't know whether it was part of the design of the jacket or whether it had been sewn on, but it reminded me of the children's book character Thomas the Tank Engine. It seemed incongruous on a man of his age. Every now and then, when he walked close by me, I noticed

5

that there was the faint smell of grease or some kind of industrial oil about him, but it was nothing too strong or unpleasant. He was not dirty, but grubby in the way someone might be who had taken half an hour off work in an industrial workplace. Little and grubby just about sums it up – there was nothing at all unusual or memorable about him.

When he asked me about the house I realised he was not from the Birmingham area. He had a softer, northern accent which I could not place – Yorkshire or Lancashire perhaps. We stood in the kitchen. He asked if I had a key to the back door but I had left it at the office. I noticed he was carrying some sort of property guide; I could see that there were several small pictures of houses on the uppermost page which he kept glancing down at.

When I asked if he would like to have a look upstairs, it was only for form's sake: I was convinced he wasn't interested in the house. After a while it becomes second nature to an estate agent to be able to differentiate between serious clients and 'time-wasters', as they are known in the trade, and Mr Southall, despite a few pertinent questions about the property, was definitely in the latter category. I didn't blame him at all: the house had been empty for months, it was in poor condition and would need a lot of work to make it habitable.

As I made my way upstairs Mr Southall, who was behind me, asked, 'Is that double-glazed?' I turned round to see him leaning against the window ledge on the right side of the stairway. I thought perhaps he had stopped there to catch his breath. I glanced over at the window and told him it was, continuing on up the stairs. 'This is the bathroom,' I told him, indicating a door on my right. He walked past me and into the bathroom. Meanwhile I walked into the rear bedroom and stood at the large window overlooking the back garden. I had been drawn

6

to the window on my previous visits to the house. Its size and the fact that it had an almost unrestricted view across wasteland and then over the motorway made it perfect for viewing the night sky, unspoilt by light pollution. I had recently developed a keen interest in astronomy and was thinking what a perfect place it would be to set up a telescope, when Mr Southall entered the bedroom. He glanced around before making his way to the two front bedrooms. Knowing that he wasn't serious I was keen to get the viewing over with, so that I could return to the warmth of the office.

I heard him walking back down the landing. I went out to join him and was about to go back down the stairs when I became aware that he had re-entered the bathroom. 'What's that up there?' he asked. I followed him and saw that he was pointing to something just above the bath. Passing him, I went up close to it to try and answer his question. 'It's just a little hook,' I said. 'Probably something to hang your flannel on.'

The smile on my face froze as I turned to face him. Physically, he had completely changed. He was somehow bigger: the grubby, innocuous little man of moments before now seemed to take up all the space in the bathroom, and he was filled with anger. In one hand he was brandishing a sort of home-made knife with a blade about nine inches long. A dirty bandage was tied around the area where the handle would normally have been. In the other hand he clenched a long, flat chisel or file, about twelve inches long. He sneered at me and, in a voice much louder, deeper and harsher than before, he snarled, 'All right.'

I stared at him in total astonishment, standing perfectly still, staring as he waved these two dangerous-looking weapons in the air. Could this be the same mild-mannered chap who, only two minutes earlier, had been telling me how people who rented accommodation rarely took proper care of it? There must be some mistake. I was utterly bewildered – until he moved towards me. Then, I knew he meant business.

His teeth were clenched as he stepped forward. I screamed and instinctively put my gloved hands out and tried to grab the two weapons. I attempted to wrest the knife from his grip but it was useless. With my left hand I bent down on the chisel as hard as I could. As I did so it began to curve, slowly, until it formed a half-moon shape. He looked at me as if I had performed some sort of superhuman feat. I was surprised myself at what the increase in adrenalin had achieved but by now I knew that this act alone would not save me and I began screaming at the top of my voice. When I looked at the window I saw that it was double-glazed, like the one he had asked about earlier. Nobody outside was going to be able to hear me, however hard I screamed. At this point my attacker tried to put his hand over my mouth to shut me up. I snapped out and, catching one of his fingers between my teeth, bit down with all the power in my jaws – but still he kept coming towards me, pushing and shoving against my body until, eventually, I overbalanced and fell across the top of the bath. Realising that he had the better of me he continued furiously trying to push me right down into the bath. I resisted with all my might, finding a power in my limbs I had never before known was there. My only hope of getting away was lost if I could not stay on my feet.

Even as I struggled against him, my mind was trying to make some sense of what was going on. I haven't done anything wrong, I kept thinking – why is he doing this to me? My body was still draped over the top of the bath, my head parallel with the taps. As he again tried to push me down I put my arm out and pressed my hand against the wall, which I hoped would give me some sort of

8

leverage. Then, trying to push my body up, I caught sight of myself in the mirrored panel which ran around the bath. My long hair was dishevelled and my face was ashen but the image which overshadowed all others was of the knife with the dirty, crudely bandaged handle, pressed up against my throat.

At that moment all the struggle seemed to drain from my body. Suddenly I knew that there was no way I could overpower this man. He was bigger than me, stronger than me and he was armed. There was just no way I was going to win. 'You're in big trouble here, girl,' I said to myself, 'big trouble, and you had better calm yourself down or you're going to end up dead.' I took my hand away from the wall and allowed my upper body to flop down into the bath. The mirrored panel crashed down on top of me. My legs still dangled uselessly over the side of the bath. 'Don't kill me,' I pleaded. 'Please don't kill me.'

'Shut up. Shut up. Be quiet. Put your legs in the bath,' he shouted.

I slid my legs into the bath and tried to speak with a calmness I certainly did not feel.

'All right, all right, calm down – you've got me,' I said quietly, hoping that my unsteady but reasonable tone of voice would help diffuse his anger. 'Remember I'm human!' The words were not entirely original. Years earlier I had read a book by Dr Miriam Stoppard, some sort of girls' guide to growing up, in which she gave advice on how to behave if threatened or attacked. 'Keep calm. Don't panic or it will make him panic and he may harm you even more. Remind him that you are human,' she had written.

'Please don't kill me,' I begged again.

'No one's going to kill you,' he hissed. 'You're not going to be harmed. Now lie still.'

I didn't believe him. What other reason could there

possibly be for this attack? I didn't know the man, I had never done anything to harm him. Only killing me seemed to make any sense at that moment.

I suddenly felt an unpleasant wet warmth and, looking down, saw that my right glove was covered in blood. During the pushing and shoving, before I had over-balanced, the sharp blade had slashed through my leather glove and cut deeply into the soft flesh of my palm, just below my index finger. There was so much blood that I thought my hand must almost have been cut off. The sight of it, oozing out of my glove, made me feel weak.

'Put your hands together,' he instructed. I did so.

After crossing them over each other he took a piece of what looked like washing-line rope from his pocket and began to bind them together. When the operation was complete he put a pair of glasses on my face. The lenses were thick, dark plastic; it was very difficult to see any-thing. 'Right, get out of the bath,' he said sharply.

I tried to struggle to my feet but with my hands tied together it was no easy task. At the third attempt I man-aged to stand up but as I did so the dark glasses, which were miles too big, slid right off my face and clattered into the bath. I looked down at them and saw that they were lying amid large chunks of my hair. He quickly snatched them up and put them back on my face.

'Where are your car keys?' he demanded. For a brief instant, relief washed over me. My God, so that's what this is all about – he wants the car. Although, even as I thought it, I knew it wasn't really plausible: nobody in their right mind would go to these lengths to get their hands on a second-hand Ford Escort.

'They're downstairs,' I said, although I knew they were in my pocket. It suddenly occurred to me that if we went to look for them I might have some chance of escape. But he didn't take the bait. I knew then for sure that he didn't want the car. There were only two possibilities left: he was either going to rape me, or kill me, or both.

The horror of my situation struck me like a blow. I was hardly able to breathe with fear. I could hear my heart thumping crazily and the blood pounding through my head. Perhaps I could beg for my freedom. 'Please . . .' I began, turning my face towards him, although because of the dark glasses he was little more than a shape before my eyes.

'Don't look at me!' he yelled, pulling my scarf from around my shoulders and tying this too around my already tightly bound wrists.

He then placed a noose of what felt like washing-line rope around my neck. It was not tied tightly but I was aware of it being repeatedly tugged on. Now I was terri-fied because of the noose round my neck. I wondered if he planned to hang me. Clearly, tied up as I was, there was little prospect of escape. I just knew that I couldn't afford to anger or excite this man any more than I already had.

'The car keys,' I said, 'they are in my pocket.' I felt it was only a matter of time before he was going to discover them anyway: perhaps my confession would convince him that I was prepared to cooperate. Whatever he had in mind I had no chance of fighting my way out. I could only hope to reason with him. Without a word he removed the keys and positioned himself behind me.

'Right, we're going downstairs,' he said. Then, putting a hand on each of my shoulders, he steered me towards the top of the stairs. As we descended he continued to guide me from behind. Because of the dark glasses I couldn't see a thing: I had to negotiate each stair separately, feeling for the edge with my foot before stepping down. The glasses kept slipping down my nose. I tried to push them back up to my face with my bound wrists. He must have noticed me doing this because he said approvingly: 'Yes, that's right, keep the glasses on.'

He told me when I had reached the bottom step, and instructed me to sit down. I was still having problems with the glasses, which continued to slip down my nose. I couldn't resist glancing at him, though God knows what made me do it; I didn't want to see him – it must have been some kind of nervous reaction.

'I told you not to look at me!' he yelled angrily. 'Keep your eyes shut!' Shocked by what I had done, I immediately looked towards my feet and pushed the glasses back up my face.

'I'm going to have to rip your scarf,' he said. I felt him untying it from around my wrists and heard the sound of tearing, before he removed the dark glasses from my face and blindfolded me. The blindfold was tight but not uncomfortable. He told me to open my mouth and when I did so, he place a rolled-up piece of material inside. He then put a piece of cloth over my mouth, which was folded and secured in exactly the same way as the blindfold. The sensation of a double gag was very unpleasant. The gag inside my mouth had a nasty bitty texture, which made me think it was some sort of industrial stuff, and tiny fragments of it started coming off in my mouth, making me fear that I would want to cough. How would I be able to cough with the secondary gag holding the first one in place? I would choke to death. Another piece of material was put over my head and secured beneath my chin like a headscarf.

He then turned his attentions to tying my legs. With what I believe was another piece of washing-line rope he encircled my legs, once, just below my knees.

'Is that too tight?' he asked. 'Stand up and try to walk.'

I took a few tottering steps.

'Is that the best you can do?'

I nodded.

He sat me back down on the stairs and I felt him loosen the rope. He took my right elbow and guided me to my feet.

'Keep walking and keep quiet,' he told me as we passed along the hallway and into the lounge. I could feel a slight pressure on the ligature as we walked, slowly, through the french windows which he had fumbled to unlock and down the garden. He was behind me all the time, pushing and guiding me. I walked as slowly as he would allow, hoping against hope that someone would see us. It couldn't be much later than 11 am – surely there must be someone looking out of their back window. In the distance I could hear the impersonal roar of motorway traffic; closer at hand I could hear birds in the surrounding gardens. Surely someone must see me. This couldn't happen in broad daylight, without someone coming to my rescue. But no one did.

It was a terrible dilemma. One part of me was wondering what the hell I was doing, just waiting, praying for someone to see me. Surely I should be screaming and shouting, trying to attract attention. Yet all the time I could feel the blade of the knife pressing between my inner arm and my ribcage as he guided me along the pathway, and the fear that he would, as he had threatened, use it if I made any rash moves, kept me compliant.

·2·

A S WE MADE our way down the path I tried to recall from previous visits where the garage was, but before I had got my bearings I realised we were inside it.

'There's a car, there, get in,' he said as he manoeuvred me towards the front passenger seat. A car – that threw me completely: obviously we were leaving Turnberry Road. Whatever was going to happen to me wasn't going to happen to me there. Suddenly the awful realisation came to me that the minute we left this address I would be completely alone. Eventually, someone would come looking for me. But if I had gone, then no one would know what had happened or have any clue as to my whereabouts.

I knew it was imperative not to leave the house, yet even as the thought went through my mind I was swinging my legs into the footwell of the car, as he had told me to. The seat was reclining at an angle of about 175 degrees. I was practically lying down as he closed the passenger door and got into the driver's seat. I felt a line of rope being secured under my chin; running from left to right it prevented me from leaning forward or making any sudden head movement.

I felt vulnerable and exposed – gagged and blindfolded, with a noose around my neck, bound hand and foot, laid out almost flat and prevented from moving my head. What sort of a weirdo was I dealing with here? Was this part of it, I wondered, to truss me up like this? I could think of no motivation for the attack other than sexual. I didn't know the man, had never seen him before in my life. I hadn't done anything bad to anyone. And yet it had clearly been planned: people don't walk about with weapons, dark glasses and lengths of rope in their pockets on the offchance.

His car had been parked here all along, all the time I had been showing him around the house, all the time he had been asking me about double-glazing and damp-coursing and I had been thinking about astronomy. I was petrified. I wondered if he intended to rape me here, in the garage, now that he had me completely immobilised. And then what? He had told me not to look at him but I had; I had seen his face. Would he kill me after he had raped me? Was this it?

A thousand thoughts came and went during the course of those few minutes, most of which I cannot remember. The only memory that is crystal clear is the feeling of absolute panic of the unknown.

Every week we read about things in the newspapers or hear things on the news that appal us, about acts of violence or cruelty. Events that, as normal human beings, we are at a loss to comprehend. Children being abused, old people being raped and robbed, animals starving to death through neglect. We shake our heads, unable to understand why anyone would do such a thing. In those few minutes every evil, abusive act I had ever heard about went through my mind and I wondered if something similar was going to happen to me.

My face was covered with a piece of light material, then

with a lightweight blanket and, finally, with what felt like a thin jacket or coat which appeared to have sleeves dangling down on either side of my head. He placed some sort of heavy, metal toolbox on my lap.

'This won't be on you for very long,' he said. 'It's just to make sure you stay down.' After securing the whole lot in place with the seatbelt, he pulled the flap of my coat to one side and I felt the by now familiar cold, sharp, metal blade press against my skin.

'Is that your stomach?'

I nodded.

'Right then, we know where we are. Don't make any moves or I'll use this.'

I nodded again. The car pulled out of the garage and made a left turn on to the dirt track alongside 153 Turnberry Road. With the weight on my face I felt as if I was suffocating. I shook my head from side to side and through the gag tried to tell him I couldn't breathe.

'Why not?' he demanded, pulling the gag to one side.

'The coat's fallen down over my face,' I told him.

'How do you know it's a coat?'

'Because it feels like a coat!' I snapped, annoyed by his question.

'Oh, you're clever as well!' he sneered. I realised I had made a serious error of judgement. My sarcastic retort had ruffled him and I didn't want that. I must not anger this man or annoy him in any way, since all the power lay in his hands. I must be careful not to give him any excuse to abuse it. But he did adjust the coat, which made breathing a little easier.

I tried to take in every detail of the drive, initially marking every right and left turn, every stop at what I imagined must be traffic lights or zebra crossings. When I finally managed to get away from this crazy man I wanted to know where I was, or at the very least to be able to explain,

17

in detail, what had happened and where he had taken me. Every time the car stopped or slowed down I could hear people around me, people going about their everyday business, walking, shopping, talking, just a few feet away on the pavement. I could scream now, I thought to myself, or I could try to struggle and fight and somebody out there might notice what was going on. Yet in my heart of hearts I knew it was hopeless. I was gagged with a double gag and trussed up like an oven-ready chicken. And above all else I knew he still had the knife somewhere close. I couldn't see it, I couldn't feel it or touch it but I knew it was there, and the thought of him using it was even more terrifying than my fear of the unknown. My body was shaking uncontrollably. I couldn't keep a limb still as the car continually stopped, started and moved slowly off through the traffic: each time felt like a missed opportunity.

Eventually, the route became less congested. We were travelling at around forty miles an hour but by this time I had no idea where we were. Fright had long since put an end to my attempts to recall every right or left turn on the route. For a time I knew we were heading south because, even through the coat, I could feel the sun on my face and, being keen on astronomy, I knew that at that time of day the sun was in the south. It wasn't very long, however, before we made another turn and although I tried to map our route I had lost the sun and my sense of direction.

It seemed we drove for ages before he pulled into what felt like a large, enclosed space and turned off the engine. I could hear the noise of traffic in the distance but where we were parked there were no fumes or movement. I think we were in a large, open air car park.

He pulled my own coat away from my body and I felt a hard pressure against my stomach that I knew immediately was the bandaged knife.

'Can you feel that?' he asked unnecessarily, as I flinched.

'Yes.'

'Do you know what it is?'

'Yes.'

'Right then, don't move. I'm going to keep that there and we are going to make a tape,' he continued.

Make a tape. I repeated his words silently in my head. Had I heard him correctly, a tape?

'You have probably realised by now that you have been kidnapped,' he said, as he lifted the toolbox from my lap and made other adjustments to my bonds.

Kidnapped? His words really didn't make a lot of sense to me. Kidnapping was something I associated with the rich and famous or television programmes like *Dallas*. It certainly wasn't something that happened to twenty-five-year-old Birmingham estate agents, I felt fairly sure about that. You had to be rich to be kidnapped, otherwise there was nobody to pay the ransom. I had no money. Mum and Dad had no money: they owned their own home but that was it. My Dad was a coach fitter and Mum worked in the local supermarket, so if this chap thought he had nabbed an heiress he was definitely on the wrong track.

As I pondered this thought, he continued to fiddle about, first removing the coat from my face and then the gag from across my mouth.

'Don't scream, I'm warning you now that if you do, this goes into you,' he said, jerking the knife blade against my stomach. I nodded and he took the rolled gag from inside my mouth. The blindfold remained in place.

'We are going to make a tape to send to your boss,' he told me.

So that was his plan. He didn't think Mum and Dad would pay the ransom. This wasn't a case of mistaken identity: he thought Shipways, who are owned by a big insurance group, would pay up. The whole improbable idea of being kidnapped began to make more sense.

'What's your name?'

'Stephanie, Stephanie Slater,' I responded.

'You can call me Bob. It's not my real name but it will do for now.'

He held what must have been a microphone to my mouth and instructed:

'Right, you're going to say exactly what I say. Repeat after me: "It's 11.35 am, this is Stephanie Slater."'

I repeated his words but he was clearly having problems with the tape recorder. First the volume wasn't working, then he recorded the sound of his own voice. By the time he had managed to sort things out for a third attempt, the message was timed at 11.45 am.

I wasn't allowed to sit up to make the tape, I just turned my head towards the microphone 'Bob' held towards my mouth. I cannot recall exactly what information my taped message contained. I was so anxious to get it right and not to make him angry again that I paid hardly any attention to the actual words he told me to speak. I only remember that there were details of a map reference and mention of a place called Burnley.

When the message was complete he put the tape in an envelope which he asked me to run my tongue along. He mentioned that he had forgotten to leave a message in the house at Turnberry Road but since I had heard some sort of scribbling on paper, I assumed he had put a note in with the tape. At this point he re-gagged me with both gags, and told me not to speak or move. He was about to get out of the car door when he noticed a passerby.

'Aye up, there's a chap over there,' he said quietly.

He quickly pulled the car door closed and threw a blanket over my head and body. He was silent and completely still, I imagine watching the movements of the man in the rear view mirror.

At last somebody had noticed us, had thought there was something suspicious going on; perhaps even at this moment he was walking towards the car to check it out. I would not make a move until the stranger appeared at the car but the minute I heard his voice, despite the gags, the ropes and even the knife, I would shout and wriggle for all I was worth. I wouldn't let another opportunity pass me by. I strained to hear the stranger's footsteps approach but the rhythmic thud of my own heartbeat drowned out all other sounds. My muscles tensed as I waited.

'It's all right, he's going,' he said quietly, almost reassuringly. 'Yes, he's gone.'

Once again he opened the car door and I heard gravel crunch beneath his feet.

'I'm just going to post this tape and I have a phone call to make. I won't be long,' he said, before closing the door behind him.

Disappointment engulfed me. Nobody had seen me, nobody was coming. I was on my own, on my own with a man I didn't know, in a place I didn't know, going God knows where. I don't know how long he was gone, all I could think about was the hopelessness of it all.

It wasn't until he got back into the car that I realised he hadn't even bothered to lock it.

I was hardly aware of leaving the car park – my hands were shaking and my stomach was turning over. It was becoming clear to me that the whole operation had been strategically planned. This had been no chance meeting: he had fixed up the appointment to view the house last week, and he had everything he needed to keep me subdued on the journey – ropes, tool box, coat, blankets and the knife. Then there was the tape recorder, all ready in the car for use at the first stop. And he claimed to have posted the tape to Shipways. 'That's that done,' he had said when he returned to the car. 'Kevin Watts will have that in the morning.' If he knew Kevin was my boss, he must have done some research.

Until minutes before I had believed I was going to be raped or murdered or both – there seemed no other logical explanation. Now things had totally changed. I so desperately wanted to believe that everything would be all right that I snatched at every crumb of hope he offered. I tried frantically to recall exactly what he had asked me to say on the tape. I remembered he had been fumbling around with some sort of map, which he would shuffle about before reading out reference numbers, numbers that he told me to repeat on the tape. He had kept clicking a hand-held microphone on and off as he relayed his instructions to me. 'I'm okay and I'm unharmed,' I recalled saying at the beginning of the message, 'and providing these instructions are carried out I will be released on . . .'

On what, on what? Oh God, he had told me to repeat the date that he planned to release me and I couldn't remember what it was. Had he said Friday? I was sure he had, Friday the 31st, that was the date he had told me to repeat. When was Friday? Today was Wednesday January the 22nd, so Friday was a couple of days away. But that would only be the 24th. I was horrified by the result of my mental calculations. He couldn't be thinking of keeping me until January 31st! It was completely crazy; what on earth was he going to do with me for nine days? I wanted to believe I had made a mistake but at the back of my mind was the awful certainty that I hadn't.

The traffic had become much lighter. We seemed to be driving along open roads or dual carriageways for about an hour before Bob stopped the car again. It felt as though he had just pulled into the side of the road, rather than into a lay-by. When he turned off the engine and simultaneously the radio went off, I realised we were at a quiet spot. It felt like open countryside. The air seemed clean and sweet and birds were singing. Only very occasionally did another vehicle pass us.

'I'm going to have a bit of lunch,' he told me. 'Do you want a ham sandwich?'

'No thank you,' I tried to say, despite the gags inside and over my mouth. I retched at the very thought. I have been a vegetarian for most of my adult life and in any case I had no intention of lying practically horizontal in the front seat of a car, bound and blindfolded, eating sandwiches with this man as if we were enjoying some sort of bizarre picnic together.

'Are you sure?' He sounded almost concerned. 'It's a long drive.'

Again I refused.

'We're going to have to kill a bit of time,' he told me. 'I don't want to arrive where we are going until about six o'clock. If you don't want a sandwich, what about a drink of tea?'

I heard the sound of liquid being poured from a container before he pulled the scarf from my face and took the rolled gag out of my mouth. He held a small plastic cup to my lips. The tea was hot, strong and very sweet. I accepted his offer of chocolate and he put a piece in my mouth.

For the seven or eight minutes it took him to eat his sandwiches in silence, I listened to the sounds outside the car. There seemed to be quite a few trains passing by and because the noise of them was so loud I guessed they were very close. The sound came from in front and above the car, as if they were travelling over a bridge above the road.

After finishing his sandwiches Bob asked if I needed to use the toilet. I refused. I couldn't imagine what sort of arrangement going to the loo would entail but I felt pretty certain he was not going to escort me to a nearby public lavatory and wait outside. He was a complete stranger – surely he didn't expect me to have a pee in the grass while he stood watching?

'We have a long journey ahead of us,' he warned.

'No, I'm all right.'

'I'll have to help you go to the toilet, if not now, later. Don't let modesty stop you. If you have any modesty now, you won't have by the time you leave me, because I'm going to be the one taking care of you. So, forget your modesty,' he continued in a light-hearted manner. 'I've got to babysit you for the next eight days.' With that he got out of the car and went round to open the boot. I heard him moving things about behind me and realised we were in a hatchback of some kind.

Eight days, he had said. I couldn't help thinking that incredible though it seemed, there might just be some truth in this kidnap story. Since the fight in the house, which had been very frightening, he had not done anything to hurt me. He had threatened me with the knife, even pushed it up against my body, but his offer of food seemed to indicate that he didn't want me to come to any harm, which would make sense if he was planning to exchange me for a ransom. I kept turning the possibilities over in my mind. I couldn't be sure of anything.

Outside, he was rubbing something over the car quite vigorously. The car was shaking with the motion of it and I could hear the squeak of the material on glass. For about ten or fifteen minutes he was out there, rubbing intermittently. I was racking my brains trying to work out where we might be but concluded it could be almost anywhere. I was completely disorientated by now.

All time I lay pondering, I was becoming increasingly and uncomfortably aware of a nagging ache in the pit of my stomach. I badly needed the loo. Maybe it was his warning that we still had a long way to go; maybe it was what my Mum had always referred to as my 'nervous stomach'. Whatever the reason, I knew I wouldn't be able to hold on for much longer.

The car door opened and he got into the driver's seat. 'That's it,' he said proudly. 'That's my disguise got rid of. They'll never recognise me.'

Any concern I might have had about him covering his tracks was superseded by my intense discomfort. 'I do need to go to the toilet,' I muttered.

'Just a minute.'

He came round to the passenger door to untie my legs and help me out of the car. The ropes around my hands were still in place, as were the blindfold and the gag. He took my arm and walked me round to the back of the car, then on to some sort of a grassy verge where, I suppose, I was out of sight of the road.

'You'll have to go here,' he said. 'You're on grass.'

In an effort to stave off the bitterly cold January weather I was wearing a heavy, black, calf-length woollen coat, over a blouse, jacket, calf-length corduroy skirt and an underskirt. With knee-length boots as well, I knew it would be almost impossible to conduct this operation with any dignity, especially since I still had my gloves on and my right hand, which had tried to grab the knife, was stinging painfully.

He stood in front of me and pulled my coat up at the back from the hem. I lifted my skirt as best I could at the front and somehow managed to get my tights and knickers down with my bound hands. Just as, perspiring heavily despite the cold, I had completed this monumental feat, I heard a train in the distance. He heard it too. He grabbed me beneath the arms and started to hurry me backwards towards the open car door.

'Quiet, quiet,' he kept repeating, although I wasn't making any noise.

I think an element of hysteria overtook me at this point. I couldn't help thinking how we would look if we were spotted by any of the people travelling on the train about to cross the bridge above us. Like a pair of dancing drunks, I thought, with him frantically shuffling backwards and me, blindfolded, lurching all over the place with my tights and drawers around my ankles. I was just as terrified at that point as I had been minutes earlier: my hands were shaking and my stomach was churning with the pain of fear, but as I fell back on to the car seat, I giggled. My God, what was happening to me, was I cracking up?

As soon as the train passed we tried again. 'All right, come on. Out you come now.'

We walked back in the same direction, behind the car and over the grassy verge. He pulled up the back of my coat again; my tights and knickers were still down. I crouched in the grass. It was difficult to balance with my hands tied together, so he held on to my shoulders while I held on to one of his legs. Despite my best efforts there was nothing I could do: the moment I started to pee I also had a sudden attack of diarrhoea. I was mortified. I tried to stand up but that only made things worse. I waited, resigned, half-crouching, half-standing, for what seemed like an age, until it was over.

'Stay where you are,' he said, as I made a move to straighten up. Then, walking behind me, while still holding my coat aloft, I felt him wipe me, my genitals and anus, with some sort of soft material or rag. He was trying to clean me up. I stood motionless like a child caught short on a day's outing, while he attempted to scrape the worst of it off my buttocks and legs. I burned with embarrassment.

After a couple of minutes of this he helped me back to the car. While I sat in the seat with my feet out of the car he attempted to wipe the shit from my boots. We didn't speak. I had never in my life experienced such humiliation. But far from being chastened by the incident I was very angry. How dare this man, a perfect stranger, subject me to this treatment, scaring me quite literally shitless and then expecting me to crouch down in a field like an animal, holding on to his leg in order to avoid falling over? 'You bastard, you bastard,' was all I could think as he started the car up again and put a tape into the cassette player. Accompanied by the Beach Boys we continued our journey.

He drove at about fifty miles an hour for the next hour or so. We didn't have much conversation although he asked me a number of questions about my height and shoe size, which I thought a bit strange. I remember him commenting on the scenery. 'I bet you don't get hills like this in Birmingham,' he said – which, considering that I was blindfolded and covered by several coats and blankets, seemed even odder. I was completely unaware of any fluctuations in the gradient of the road and wondered if perhaps the comment had been meant to confuse me, in case I was trying to chart where we were. He needn't have bothered. We could have been in Wales or Woking for all I knew.

Simply because of the number of hours that had passed I felt that we must be nearing our destination, and in fact by this time I wanted to get there. Bob had mentioned a couple of times that he didn't want to arrive before dark, and I felt it must be approaching night time by now. Perhaps when we got to wherever we were going he would reveal exactly what he had in mind for me. I was terrified at the prospect yet I felt I must know. When he said he was stopping to fill up with petrol I could scarcely believe my ears. Surely he didn't intend driving into a garage with me trussed up in the front of the car? He didn't: he pulled off the road on to uneven ground and filled up with a can he had brought with him. I could smell the fumes. We then waited for about forty-five minutes, until it went dark outside, before setting off again.

Eventually I was aware of the car slowing down and taking a left turn down a bumpy dirt track which we travelled along very slowly for less than a hundred yards. Bob pulled the handbrake on roughly and switched off the engine. 'Right, we're here. Stay where you are for a minute and when you do get out, remember, no screaming. Not that anybody's going to hear you out here.'

There was the crunch of gravel as he walked away. I lay perfectly still. I strained my ears but couldn't hear a thing – no traffic, no trains, nothing. Then through the darkness there was the grating, scraping sound of metal against metal, as if a large iron door was being pulled open along iron runners. He was back. Opening the door without a word, he began to untie the ropes that prevented me from moving, leaving the ones that bound my hands and legs in place.

'Swing your legs out,' he ordered, 'and stand up.'

Standing behind me, with his hands on my shoulders, he propelled me slowly forwards. It was only a few steps but he seemed in a rush to get me inside the building. I couldn't understand why: the place gave the impression of being totally deserted. We entered a building of some kind, the ground beneath my feet changing from earth to stone or brick. With my feet still tied together, he helped me shuffle inside for a distance of some forty or fifty feet. 'Come on, you're all right,' he kept saying. 'Come on, that's right, keep walking.'

He gripped my shoulders and turned me to face the left. 'All right, that's far enough. There's a chair behind you.'

With his help I sat down gingerly on a hard wooden chair. Immediately, he secured handcuffs around my wrists and ankles and tied my arms and body to the straight-backed chair with a length of rope. When he was satisfied I was completely immobile I sensed him stand back, right behind me, and stare, probably congratulating himself on having pulled the whole thing off. Here I was, certainly hours and probably miles from the house from which I had been abducted, just as he had planned. Mission accomplished, or certainly the first part of it. Only he knew what would happen next.

I didn't move a muscle and neither of us made a sound, but my sense that his eyes were boring into the back of my head was making me very uncomfortable. I wondered whether this was it. Nobody knew where I was; he could do whatever he wanted to me now. I felt the tension in my neck and shoulders increase, as if I was bracing myself for a blow. I wanted to speak, to break the moment, but I couldn't – I was simply too frightened to formulate a sentence, a question, anything.

I felt him touch my hair. My body jerked dramatically, as if in the first stages of a fit. He said nothing but continued silently to play with my hair. He pulled it back from my face, straightening it by running his fingers through its length, pulling any loose strands towards the middle. He seemed irritated by the elasticated bobble I had used to keep it all from falling over my eyes. He was obviously trying to get it out but couldn't. I remained completely still.

'I'm going to have to cut this,' he said quietly.

I thought he meant my hair. But it was just the band he wanted removed. As he snipped it out my hair fell forward, framing my face. He carefully straightened it into the shape he wanted, pulling it back behind my ears, making sure there were no stray strands. He tied it with a piece of material that had once been part of my scarf, and stood back to admire his handiwork. 'We're going to have to change your clothes,' he said very quietly. 'It's all right, I've got some others here for you to wear.'

·3·

I JERKED MY head forward, away from his hands. It seemed to have the desired effect. 'Are you hungry?' he asked, unfastening the gag, brisk and businesslike again. 'Do you like fish and chips?'

The last thing on my mind was food, even though the piece of chocolate he had given me was all I had eaten that day, but I knew I should have something. It was essential to keep my strength up and my wits about me. I hadn't formulated any plan to escape but the thought loomed large at the edge of my consciousness. I told him I liked chips. I was afraid to mention that I was vegetarian in case he forced me to eat meat or something else that he thought would upset me. So far, he had fought with me, threatened me with a knife, almost suffocated me and repeatedly tied me up. I wasn't going to hand him on a plate the opportunity to do yet more damage.

'Right then, I'll go and get you some chips. While I'm gone don't make a sound. You can't get out of here and nobody can get in, unless they break the door down. I won't be long.'

I sat rigid with fear. He had opened and then closed the metal door, but I hadn't heard the car leave, so I couldn't

31

be sure he had even left the building. Somewhere close by a radio was playing. I recognised it as 'American Pie', by Don McClean, a song I had always liked. I thought of the many times I had sung along with it:

Bye, bye Miss American Pie
Drove my Chevy to the levee
But the levee was dry
Them good old boys were drinking whiskey and rye
Singing this will be the day that I die
This will be the day that I die . . .

I knew that if I managed to get out of this mess alive, I'd never be able to listen to the song again without recalling this moment. It was the first time since that morning that I had been left alone for more than a few minutes, the first time I had had an opportunity to take stock of what had happened.

The situation still didn't seem real. It was almost as if I had been sucked out of my real life and temporarily dropped into this one. I wondered what would be happening at Shipways now. They must have told my Mum and Dad by now, so somebody would be looking for me. Or would they? Perhaps they would think I had decided to go off on my own. I hadn't been unhappy or had a row with anyone but people seem to leave their homes and families all the time for no apparent reason. It would never be my style, though, and I was fairly sure my colleagues at Shipways and particularly my parents would know that.

If Bob had posted off the tape, as he'd said, it should arrive at Shipways tomorrow morning, then everyone would know for sure. On the long drive here, I had remembered more details of the taped message. I had said that by next Wednesday, they would need an Ordnance

Survey map for Blackburn and Burnley. And that Kevin Watts, the office manager, must be the person who acted as a courier, using his own car. Either Jane or Sylvia, my colleagues in the office, could act as guides for Kevin but there must not be more than two people in the car and the passenger must not get out at any time. The money must not be marked in any way whatsoever.

Well, that should leave them in no doubt as to what had happened, but what would they do about it? Would they think it was some sort of joke or hoax? I doubted that. I had clearly gone missing from Turnberry Road, as far as I knew, without trace. Bob had mentioned that he meant to leave a note in the house but had forgotten to do so. Not that a note would have told them where to find me. He wouldn't tell them that until he was ready. If he ever was.

I couldn't keep pushing to the back of my mind the fact that nobody would know where to begin looking for me. We had clearly driven miles since this morning and I felt we must be very far away from Birmingham. The only way I was going to be released was if he decided to let me go. I wasn't sure he could be trusted to do that, whatever he said. Miriam Stoppard's book came into my mind again: her advice had been to remind your attacker that you are human. I knew instinctively that it was my only chance. I had to be careful not to annoy him, I had to persuade him I was a human being with a family and a life I considered very precious. I had to make him know that I had a role in life other than that of kidnap victim.

There was a grating noise as he opened the door and closed it behind him. Without a word he came over to the chair and started to untie the rope around my upper body. He left in place the handcuffs on my wrists and boots. Helping me to stand, he then took hold of my shoulders from behind and propelled me slowly across the floor for a few feet.

'There's a mattress on the floor there, right behind you. I'll hold on to you while you lower yourself on to it.'

I did as he asked and ended up lying awkwardly on the mattress on my left side, with my hands and feet still uncomfortably bound. He removed the gags but left the blindfold in place. I heard him tear open the paper that contained the chips and put them down on the mattress in front of me. When he had handcuffed my wrists he'd first put on a pair of socks which he said would prevent the metal of the handcuffs cutting into my flesh. So I started to eat with the socks still over my hands. The chips were very hot and without salt or vinegar. I only managed about five – they tasted foul – but that could have had something to do with the gag that had been in my mouth for several hours. There were still bits of grit from it lodged in my throat.

'Is that all you're going to eat?' he asked me, handing me a cup of hot, sweet tea.

'Yes, I'm not very hungry.'

'Just have a few more.'

'No, really, I've had enough, thanks.'

I heard him rolling up the chip paper and tidying things away. Meanwhile, I held the tea between my handcuffed hands and sipped it gratefully. As I did so, the grit in my throat was gradually washed away by the hot liquid.

'Right, it's time we got you out of those clothes. I've got some here for you to wear,' he said.

I was frightened as he helped me off the mattress and to my feet. He hadn't explained why he wanted to change my clothes and I was too scared to ask him. But it felt wrong.

He took the handcuffs off my wrists and ankles but the blindfold remained in place. After helping me remove my coat, he took off my blouse, white T-shirt that I was wearing as a sort of vest and my bra. Finally he helped me off with my boots and skirt, underskirt, tights and knickers.

I felt horribly exposed as I stood there naked and blindfolded. I raised my arms and crossed them over my chest.

'Put your arms down!' he rapped out crossly.

Immediately I let them fall to my sides.

'Hold them out in front of you,' he instructed. As I did so I felt him clamp the handcuffs back on my wrists. It was very cold and I could feel the gooseflesh rising on my skin. I didn't know what he was doing but I could hear him breathing shallowly what seemed like only inches from my face. I was frozen with fear. Not the fear I had been experiencing since that morning: fear of the unknown. This new dread felt more like fear of the inevitable.

Without a word he began to touch me, rubbing and squeezing my breasts as I stood motionless. Then he said quietly, 'Get on the mattress.'

I didn't move. I couldn't move. I was petrified.

'Get down on the mattress,' he repeated, more firmly this time.

I lay on the mattress with my hands above my head as he had instructed. I knew there were lights on but because of the blindfold I was in darkness. I couldn't see what he was doing but it sounded as if he was getting undressed. I felt him sit on the mattress at my feet.

'Open your legs,' he said.

I parted my thighs very slightly.

'Open your legs, properly.' His voice was beginning to coarsen. I must not make him angry. Whatever happened I must not make him angry with me. I opened my legs and for several minutes lay completely still, knowing that he was scrutinising my body. I could almost feel his eyes moving over me, looking at me, assessing me. It was a despoiling act made all the more abhorrent because I couldn't see him doing it. I was being used like a pornographic magazine without having the satisfaction of being able to challenge his dirty little schoolboy antics, even with my eyes.

He asked me if I was a virgin. I told him that I wasn't. He then asked me if I was married or had any children. I said I didn't, that I lived at home with my Mum and Dad, but that I did have a boyfriend.

He put his hand on my leg. 'You're shaking,' he said, as if he was surprised. 'Why are you shaking?'

'Because I'm frightened and I'm cold,' I responded, my body making involuntary movements more akin to jerking now than shaking.

'It's not cold,' he insisted.

From that point it was almost as if I split into two separate entities, my body and my mind. My body was going to be forced to endure the things he asked of it but my mind took a step backwards and became an observer rather than a participant, watching what was going on. I was now a mere onlooker, while he was the puppet-master. My body could feel him moving over me in a strange, crablike way and feel the intense pain of him savagely and repeatedly biting my breasts, but my mind was completely empty of thoughts or feelings. I didn't even register disgust as he tried to kiss me and slobbered all over my mouth. I just cut out as he humped and grunted his way through this obscene travesty.

When it was over I felt him leave the mattress. Moments later he was back.

'Open your legs,' he instructed me again.

With a cold sponge and cold water he washed between my legs and towelled me dry.

'You don't have to worry about catching Aids,' he said informatively, 'because I was wearing something.'

After getting rid of the wet sponge he pulled me up off the mattress and handed me my knickers and an old, over-large pair of denim jeans which I put on. Over my Dad's T-shirt I pulled two jumpers. Then, before giving me back my boots, he gave me a pair of socks.

'I hope you're not claustrophobic,' he said when I was dressed.

'No, not really.'

'Good, because I'm going to put you in a box within a box and that will be where you sleep. Do you need the toilet before we get you sorted out for bed?'

I nodded. He manoeuvred me behind the mattress to where there was a bucket. 'You might want this,' he said, handing me half a roll of soft toilet paper. Because there were a couple of chain links between the right and left handcuffs I was able to unfasten the jeans and pull them and my knickers down. I wasn't aware of him watching me but the moment I had finished fastening up the jeans he was there.

'Right, you're going to bed now,' he said, matter-of-factly, in much the same tone my Dad might have used with me when I was about eight years old.

'I want you to lie down on the mattress and shuffle forward towards the box that's at the end of it, as if you were getting into a sleeping bag,' he said as he secured the other handcuffs around my feet. 'Have you got that?'

I had absolutely no idea what he was talking about or what I was supposed to be shuffling into but I did as he had asked, with him kneeling at my head. I continued to shuffle down until my hips wedged against the sides and I could go no further.

'I can't get down any more,' I said, panicking slightly because I desperately wanted to do as I had been told.

'You should be able to, I can get down it,' he said, a note of irritation in his voice.

I turned slightly on my side, so that my shoulders were now lying flat on the bottom of the box but with my hips and lower body twisted at an angle. By bending my knees slightly I managed to get the whole of my body inside. From my armpits to my ankles my body was now encased in what felt like a wooden coffin. This box was wedged into what I later discovered was a plastic wheely bin lying on its front and with the bottom cut out. My feet protruded into another encased space. I couldn't work out what this was; it could have been a hole in the wall and there appeared to be materials or rags of some kind in there. As I entered the box it didn't rock at all or move in any way; it was clearly secured to the ground. Bob had been telling the truth when he said I would be going into a box for the night – a box within a box.

As soon as I was in, he took hold of my wrists by the handcuff chain and tied them above my head to what felt like a metal bar. My elbows were extended outside the coffin and my hands were handcuffed and clasped together above my head, directly in front of my face.

'Feel this,' he said, stretching one of my fingers. I touched what felt like a stone.

'Don't pull on the bar because there are boulders above you – can you feel them?'

I nodded.

'If you pull on the bar, you'll pull them down and crush yourself. No shouting, no screaming, don't make a sound. And when I open this door in the morning I want to see the gag still on you and the blindfold still on you. Have you got that?'

'Yes, okay.'

'Now I don't know if you can feel it but there's a length of wire in the box. Can you feel it?'

38

I could feel something running the length of the coffin so I nodded again.

'That wire is attached to electrodes. If you move you will get an electric shock. So, no noise, don't pull the bar above you, in fact don't move at all, all right?'

'All right.'

'Now I'm going to close the bin lid before I go, but there are air holes in it, so you won't suffocate.'

There was a brief pause. Because I was blindfolded I couldn't see what was happening but I hadn't heard him move so I assumed he was still kneeling at my head. Perhaps he was staring at me in disbelief, because his voice sounded genuinely incredulous when he spoke.

'I can't understand why you're so calm. Why are you so calm?'

'I'm not calm,' I said, although I realised when I spoke that even my voice sounded as though I was. 'I'm frightened to death.'

I was more than relieved when he didn't put the rolled-up gag back inside my mouth; however, he secured the other one very securely across my mouth.

'Right, that's it, I'm going to close up the lid now, all right?'

'Yes.'

'See you in the morning then.' He sounded almost jaunty.

I heard the sound of a lid being drawn closed and immediately felt the space I was in reduced. I would never be able to breathe in here; there was no air. I was going to suffocate. I sucked in air desperately. My heart lurched and I felt a sob rise in my throat and break silently against the fabric of the gag.

Please, please, no. It wasn't even a whisper. Just a thought so dominating every other thought or emotion, I felt he must pick it up. Please. Don't let this happen.

But outside, oblivious or unconcerned, he was already securing the bin lid with bolts. I could hear the sound of them being shot into place.

·4·

I T WAS COLD in the box. I had managed to wriggle my thumbs underneath the blindfold and pull it up a bit, which helped relieve the aching behind my eyeballs, but it was still so dark that the blackness was almost a solid shape in front of my eyes.

He had definitely gone. At first, even though I had heard the noise of the car disappearing into the distance, I thought he might still be around. He could have crept back, sneaked in to watch me, or rather to watch the box. None of it made any sense anyway, so why wouldn't he come back to watch the box, to see whether I would try to escape, to listen to the boulders crashing on to my skull and the electrodes jolting through my body? For at least an hour I had listened intently to the silence, straining to hear the faint shuffle of feet or the slightest clearing of a throat, but there had been no sound. I was alone. The thought both relieved and terrified me.

At least his absence meant that for the time being there would be no violence. My hand was stiff and sore where his knife had cut into it during the struggle in the bathroom. My breasts were stinging painfully from his repeated biting. I didn't even want to think about that part of it: I knew I had to put it behind me or I would crack up completely.

In the car he had said that he would be babysitting me for eight days. I had to be positive. It was a long time but I could survive it. No I couldn't, I couldn't survive another eight minutes of this, never mind eight days. Eight days is a lifetime – people go for exotic holidays for less time than that.

I had seen it in the paper at work only a couple of days earlier. A seven-day cruise down the Nile for under £300. I'd looked out of the window on to a typical grey, bitterly cold winter's day in Great Barr and thought how wonderful it sounded. And while I was wedged into this bloody torture chamber, I thought, somebody, somewhere is about to set off on the holiday of a lifetime. I shifted my back; it was beginning to ache really badly now, and my feet were like blocks of ice.

What on earth made him think my employers would pay any money for me? It was crazy, he was obviously a madman. Kidnap? Ransom? He must think this is *Dallas* or *Dynasty*: that's the only place anyone kidnaps anyone, on television. Perhaps the kidnap story was just a ploy to keep me quiet: if you behave yourself and do as I say, I will let you go, if you don't I'll kill you.

What was stopping him from killing me anyway, when he had finished with me? If it was, as he said, a kidnap for a ransom, then why had he raped me? I would have thought he would want to take better care of someone he planned to exchange for money. If, on the other hand, he had always intended to rape me, then why hadn't he let me go, or killed me straight afterwards?

The horrible thought entered my mind that he might have plans to keep me around as a sort of captive sex toy, to be pulled out of the box and used at his convenience. I knew this was a possibility but I was too fragile, emotionally, to confront it. I could not yet allow myself to think about the details of the rape; it was simply too much to face on top of everything else. Each time a picture of what had happened came back to me I froze it out, filed it away in my subconscious, to be dealt with later.

For a long period I just lay motionless, without a thought in my mind, staring into the blackness. I have never enjoyed being on my own. I'd never spent an entire night alone in all my twenty-five years: there had always been my Mum or Dad, a relative, friend or boyfriend, if not actually in the room with me, at least somewhere in the house. I was more alone than I had ever been in my life, and I was scared. What if he didn't come back? Perhaps this was all part of his sick plan, to leave me here in this box, unable to move or make a sound. Whatever he had done to me, whatever he intended to do, was preferable to being left here alone to die.

I gingerly tried to shift my position. Even the fear of the boulders and the electrodes was fading as the numbing cold spread through my body. As the night wore on I felt as if I was lying in snow. Every inch of my body ached but the pain in my back – I have always had back problems – was absolutely excruciating. Pains were also shooting through my arms, which remained suspended above my head, and through my legs. By now I couldn't feel my feet at all, they were so cold. I felt I should cry but I didn't. I knew that if I was going to get through this ordeal, whatever form it might take and however long it might go on, I would have to be strong. That was my only chance.

If my sense that I was in some sort of workshop was correct then I reckoned that there must be tools or at least metal objects around the place. If and when Bob returned, I would try to get him to untie my hands, then I would pick something up and clobber him with it. So far I had been completely compliant, so he wouldn't be expecting trouble – I would have the advantage of surprise. I tried to become so absorbed in my thoughts of escape that I could block out the pains and the cold. I had stopped shivering hours ago and I lay stiffly, with the cold enveloping me like a large overcoat. In some strange way I had relaxed into it; only the sudden spasms that emanated from my lower back and ricocheted around my body and through my limbs convinced me that I was still conscious. This must be what hypothermia feels like, I thought; eventually I will become completely apathetic and slip into a coma. I had always believed that nature took over when a certain level of pain had been reached. That's what happens in the movies: the pain becomes intolerable and the hero or heroine passes out into merciful oblivion. I'm not sure if that was what happened to me but at the worst point of the night something strange and mystical happened that I am at a loss to explain.

I have never been a religious person. I believe in God but I'm no church-goer: weddings and christenings are about it. Any interest I have had in churches has been historical rather than spiritual – I love beautiful old buildings. I cannot recall my particular thoughts as I lay in the blackness. I was certainly in pain and frightened, and the dark compounded my fear. To open your eyes and see absolutely nothing but blackness is a terrible experience. Even when you are asleep in bed, if you suddenly wake and open your eyes, you can see a street-light through the curtains or something, but this was total blackness.

Suddenly, from what looked like the distance, I saw a speck of light; at first no bigger than a tiny coin, it gradually came closer and closer. As it moved into focus, sometimes moving very slightly from side to side, I realised it

44

was a face I recognised. I had seen it before in a church at Godshill on the Isle of Wight. It was the face of Christ as depicted on the Cloth of Veronica. The original Cloth of Veronica, which is in the Vatican, is believed to be the piece of material used by a sympathetic onlooker to wipe the sweat from Christ's face as he carried his cross to Calvary; it is said to carry a perfect imprint of his features and spots of his blood, caused by the crown of thorns. The one in Godshill is a copy but from the moment I first saw it I had found it completely mesmerising, and presumably I had retained it in my subconscious.

I knew it was a picture – I didn't think it was Christ visiting me in the box – and yet in a strange way I did, because it was exactly how I had pictured him since childhood. There were no shoulders or torso, just the disembodied face coming towards me, with longish hair, full mouth, and eyes not really open or closed. There are some fairly gory religious pictures of the crucifixion around but the face I saw before me that night was beautiful, and so real that I felt that if I had been able to reach out and touch it, it would have felt warm beneath my fingers.

People will interpret my 'vision' in different ways. It seems probable that the picture in Godshill Church struck such a chord with me when I first saw it that I recalled it again in an unprecedented moment of mental and spiritual anguish. I was desperate for something to believe in; everything, everyone, it seemed, had deserted me. The picture was so vivid that it filled me with a strange feeling of tranquillity. Although I remember smiling, I really believed at that moment that I was going to die, and the feelings of cold and pain that had been so immense had vanished.

I recalled reading accounts of near-death experiences in which people had experienced the feeling of passing through a bright tunnel or doorway and I searched the darkness around the vision's head for a brightly lit exit to go through but there was nothing, just blackness all around him – no doors, no lights, no tunnels. I remember being filled with sadness. Miraculously, though, the pain had gone and in a little while the vision began to fade, moving further and further back into the distance until it had completely disappeared. At last I fell asleep.

By the morning all thoughts of escape had gone. I couldn't move, let alone struggle for freedom: my whole body was a mass of aching and hurting. My arms, which had been suspended in the air above my face all night, had locked into position. Although at one level the pain in them was excruciating, at another level I couldn't feel them at all. I had read about people who have had a limb amputated and who believe they can still feel pain in it. I hadn't taken it seriously at the time but I could now easily imagine it.

I became aware of music playing: somewhere fairly close by a radio had come on. So, he had come back. Whatever else, he didn't intend to leave me in this box to rot. It sounds crazy but I was filled with feelings of relief and gratitude. This man had attacked me, kidnapped and raped me before forcing me into a cold, dark, airless box where I had spent the night twisted and wracked with pain. But he was the only person in the world who knew where I was. I was totally at his mercy for my survival and, thank God, he had returned.

I remembered that I had managed to push the blindfold up a little way during the night and slide the gag down. I frantically attempted to hook my stiff, cold thumbs, both completely devoid of feeling, beneath the material of the blindfold, to hitch it back over my eyes. I couldn't make either my fingers or my thumbs work. I jabbed my nose and my cheek repeatedly as I tried to locate my eyes. Somehow I managed it, and then slipped the gag up and into my mouth. Outside, the radio was turned down and I heard Bob walk up to the bin.

'Are you awake?' he asked through the still-fastened lid.

'Yes,' I replied through the gag. It came out as a croaky mumble.

'Have you got your blindfold on?'

'Yes.'

It took just a few moments to draw back the bolts and open the lid of the bin but it seemed like an hour or more. Suddenly there was a rush of crisp, cold air and, even through the blindfold, I could detect a change in the light: it was morning. If the devil himself had poked his head in at that moment I would have been grateful for the company. Bob was clearly not a normal man. He had carefully planned and executed this crime. I had no reason to trust him and every reason to hate and despise him, yet I experienced only joy as the bin lid opened and I heard him gruffly say:

'Come on, then, out you come!'

I had got through the night, I hadn't died and he had, as he'd promised, returned. Maybe I could get through this. He unfastened the handcuffs from the bar above my head, and as he did so my hands and arms fell on to my chest like two lead weights. There was no feeling in them at all.

'Come on, just shuffle out this way,' he instructed.

'I can't,' I mumbled as he removed the gag.

'What do you mean?'

I tried to keep the panic out of my voice. 'I can't move my arms, I can't get out. I'm sorry, I can't move them, they're completely numb.'

He didn't say anything but reached inside the box and took hold of me under my arms and dragged me slowly out. He then helped me up from the mattress and on to the hard-backed chair. The gag was removed but the blindfold stayed in place. As he moved about the workshop I tentatively clenched and unclenched my fists, trying to get rid of the numbness in my hands. Try as I might, I could not straighten my arms, which were twisted up in front of me. He didn't say a word; I think he was probably shocked by the state I was in. I began to feel a slight tingling in my elbows and arms but the dominant sensation throughout my body was one of intense pain.

'Here,' he said, 'here's a cup of tea for you.'

'I can't hold it,' I told him. 'I can't feel anything.'

'Come on, you can,' he said, pushing a mug into my twisted hands where, miraculously, it balanced and remained upright.

'They'll be all right. Have a drink,' he instructed.

I tried to lower my mouth to the mug since I knew that raising the mug was out of the question.

Bob clearly thought I was over-reacting to what was basically just a bit of stiffness in my elbows and tried to push my hands, which were clasped around the mug, towards my lips. A series of pains shot through my arms like lightning bolts.

I could not contain a loud groan. It was agony.

He dropped his hands and although he said nothing I felt he was staring at me intently.

'You can't move them at all?' he asked.

'No, not at all.'

'Right then, come here,' he said quietly.

He took the mug from my hands and very gently began to rub my elbows and inner forearms. This continued for several minutes and helped ease the pain a little. When he stopped he said, 'There, is that any better?'

'Yes, much better, thank you.'

'Don't thank me!' he snapped. For no reason I could understand he sounded angry. 'You've got nothing to thank me for.'

I sat back against the chair. No, I don't suppose I have, you crazy bastard, I thought to myself. If it wasn't for you I wouldn't be here in the first place. But as a child I had been taught to be polite. How many times had I heard my Mum say: 'Good manners cost nothing, Stephanie.' Old habits die hard. I was simply operating the code of behaviour I had lived with all my life: if you want something you say please, if you get it you say thank you. He may not have liked it, but it is part of the person I am. As far as I could see, by continuing to employ that same code of behaviour, by remaining polite, cooperative and communicative, I might just be able to convince this man of my humanity and in that way save my life.

At Turnberry Road I had seen a side to Bob that I wouldn't forget in a hurry. When I went along with his wishes he was calm and unruffled, sometimes seeming quite concerned about my welfare. But when I struggled against what he wanted he had become violent and hurt me. I had been aware of this the night before when he'd raped me. I knew what he was going to do and I didn't try to stop him.

Was that consent? I didn't shout or scream or even try to push him away from me. I had just lain there frozen, and let him get on with it – which is exactly what he had done. It hadn't been a frenzied rape, it hadn't been sadistic. It was humiliating and emotionless, devoid of any sort of sexuality. I didn't understand it or him, especially since this morning he was like a different person, making me tea and rubbing my stiffened arms and elbows. What was it all about? Only minutes ago, when he'd opened the bin, I had been euphoric; now I was desperately unhappy and confused.

'Do you want some porridge?'

'Yes.'

He moved away from the chair and I could hear him doing something just a few yards from me. In the meantime, I continued to dip my head to sip the hot, strong, sweet tea he had given me. It had been so cold in the box – I later learned that the temperature that night fell to seven degrees below freezing – and it was cold in the workshop that morning. I was as stiff and sore as if I had been beaten.

I really hate being cold; I always have. Like most of my generation I grew up with the benefits of central heating, waking up in the morning to a warm house and as much hot water as I wanted. I had laughed at my Dad's tales of when he was a lad, living with coal fires and tin baths in front of the fire. But this morning I could sympathise with what it must have been like. I was not only cold but my body and clothes were damp. There was a horrible clamminess about the workshop that seemed to hang in the air, although Bob had turned on some kind of electric heater. A short pinging sound bounced around the open space. I was to hear it many times during the following week. It was a microwave oven. This time the ping announced that my first breakfast in captivity was ready to be served.

Bob sat directly in front of me. My hands were free of the handcuffs but I was still unable to move them. He fed me porridge with a metal spoon. It was like no porridge I had ever tasted before, lumpy with bits of bran and what tasted suspiciously like wood in it – but it was hot, I was hungry and I ate it all. When it was finished he placed another mug of tea in my hands. By now I could lift my arms but for some reason I was unable to steer them to my mouth. Bob guided the mug towards my lips until I had finished.

'Right,' he said in a determined voice as he took the

empty bowl away. 'Let's get you sorted out and then I'll tell you what's going to happen.'

He unfastened the handcuffs around my boots and put what I later discovered was an ankle manacle attached to a length of chain around my right leg. It was anchored to something in the workshop but the chain was long enough to allow me to move between the box, the chair, the mattress and the makeshift toilet.

'I can see your arms are a bit stiff but how did you go on in there otherwise?' he enquired almost jauntily.

How did he think I had 'gone on'? How would anybody have 'gone on' locked up in a dark, airless coffin on a freezing cold night, bound hand and foot, gagged and blindfolded? I felt like death and knew that that was exactly how I must look, yet here was this nutter asking me how I had gone on as if I had just got back from a week in Majorca.

'I was freezing cold,' I told him, 'and I feel really sore and achy this morning.'

'Why is that?'

Why do you think, you stupid prat, I wanted to yell, but instead I mumbled in an apologetic tone, 'I think it's because the box is too small for me to be able to lie down properly. It's very tight in there. My hips got wedged and I could only lie flat on my back as far as my waist. The rest of me was just sort of jammed in at an angle. My back is killing me.'

'Mmm, I'll have to see to that, then.'

After he had helped me on to the mattress he outlined his plan. I would be kept here until next Wednesday, when he would collect a ransom of £175,000 from Shipways. He would then drive me back to the Birmingham area and tell the police where he had dropped me. There was, he assured me, no reason why, this time next week, I shouldn't be home with my Mum and Dad, if I behaved

51

myself. Behaving myself included keeping my blindfold on at all times, doing everything I was told, not attempting to shout or scream and not attempting to escape.

'We don't want to hurt you, but we will if we have to,' he concluded. 'Right, now I've got work to do, so let's get this into your mouth.' He put the hated roll of gritty material back into my mouth, which I opened without complaint, and secured it with some sort of sticky tape.

'Lie down, keep still and be quiet,' he said. He covered me with a lightweight blanket and walked away.

I didn't know where he was but the occasional bang or rattle, albeit muffled, made me think he was working in another part of the building. I was convinced it was some sort of workshop, particularly since the slight smell of oil I had noticed around Bob at Turnberry Road was stronger here. I tried to recall everything he had said to me. Today was Thursday and he said he would be keeping me here until next Wednesday. I wondered why he thought Shipways would pay £175,000 for me. What if they didn't? What if Shipways decided to say no? I hadn't worked there all that long and it was a hell of a lot of money.

I wondered if anyone had told my parents what was going on. My Mum would be going crazy by now. She had always suffered with her nerves and was already taking medication – what would this do to her? My Dad, I knew, would handle it and be a source of strength and support for Mum. He would keep everyone calm. That's if they knew what was going on. Would Shipways tell them? Did Shipways know? I only had Bob's word that the tape recording had been sent. And what did I know about Bob? Certainly nothing to inspire confidence. It bothered me that I couldn't recall exactly how he looked; I knew it would be important if I ever got out of here. I went on with my personal question and answer session for some time – it helped clarify things in my mind.

One thing that particularly puzzled me was the 'we' he had thrown into the conversation about not taking off my blindfold, screaming or trying to escape. He hadn't mentioned anyone else until that point but I was certain he had said: 'We don't want to hurt you but we will if we have to.' So he wasn't in this on his own. I wondered how many were involved and if I would meet them. The thought of others being involved made me uneasy.

I had decided, almost without having to think about it, that I would go along with this man's wishes, that I would behave myself and attempt to establish some kind of rapport with him. I could only do this by concentrating on more positive things. For instance, this morning he had shown some humanity in rubbing my elbows and feeding me. When I'd told him I couldn't move my arms he could have said, 'Tough, then you don't get any breakfast.' But he hadn't, he had been quite solicitous. I felt that I could work on developing that rapport with one person – I'd been on estate-agency training courses on the subject – but I was less confident of being able to establish a relationship with a gang. Any thoughts of what 'they' might have in store for me I had to put firmly at the back of my mind.

I had been on the mattress for a couple of hours when I heard the sound of voices. My heart missed a beat: this must be another member of the gang. I couldn't hear what they were talking about. The voices were muffled and in the distance, but there were definitely two people. I lay there half-expecting Bob to bring his mates in to see me but to my relief I heard a short ring and then silence. Then about half an hour later I heard voices again: there was a bit of banging, more talking, a ring and then silence. Suddenly it came to me. It was a shop. The ring I had heard was the sound of an old-fashioned shop till being opened. The people talking to Bob weren't members of his gang; they were customers, coming into a shop to buy things. I was being held in the back of a shop or a garage of some kind. Maybe Bob was up in the front part fixing cars while I was in the workshop behind. The two areas must be separated by some sort of wall or partition, but it must be fairly flimsy because I could hear through it.

Despite my earlier resolution not to make trouble, the possibility that I could attract the attention of somebody in the shop immediately leapt to mind. If I could work out a way of making a noise, I would be free. But what if, for some reason, Bob heard me and the customer didn't? What if I mistimed it? There were a thousand 'what ifs' to be dealt with, and the answer to all of them was the same. If it went wrong he would almost certainly kill me. His warning had been clear enough. 'We don't want to hurt you but if we have to we will.' Well, I wasn't stupid: hurting me would do no good. It must be killing me he was talking about. He might even be able to kill me and collect the ransom as well, since he had already got the taped message to Shipways out of me.

I was in an agony of indecision. One moment I would decide that the next time I heard voices I would stumble about, kick over the makeshift loo, bang into the chair and generally roar like a wounded bull. Then I would hear people talking and I would be filled with doubt. How much notice would anyone take of a bucket being kicked over or the sound of a chair falling to the floor? These are everyday noises, after all. And as for attempting to scream out loud, how much noise could I reasonably expect to make with a strip of three-inch tape over my mouth?

I was aware of Bob coming into the back part of the workshop a number of times. At one point I realised he had brought a dog in with him. He must have tied it up fairly close to the mattress because although it didn't come close enough to touch me, I could hear it panting and growling a little as it ran up and down on what sounded like a similar length of chain to the one I was now wearing. He constantly yelled at the dog to be quiet and on one occasion it sounded as if he threw a stone or a small piece of brick at it in order to make it lie still.

During the course of the day I noticed that occasionally a train passed somewhere in the distance. I could also detect the sound of cars but no more than three or four of them. I worked out that while they might be quite close they could also be miles away: perhaps I could only hear them when the wind was in the right direction. Bob had implied we were miles from anywhere when he had told me not to scream the night before. 'Not that anybody's going to hear you out here,' he had added. And judging by the wind that had whistled and howled around the building during the night, we could be on top of a mountain somewhere.

Inside the workshop Bob was sawing something with an electric saw. The noise upset the dog and the dog's whining clearly upset Bob. If he was using an electric saw I was probably not in a motor mechanic's garage, I reckoned. My notion that I was in an engineering workshop of some kind still seemed the most likely.

I lay still on the mattress for several hours after the sawing had stopped, aware of people coming in and out of the building and holding brief conversations with Bob. I dozed off at one point and when I woke I badly needed to use the loo. Through the confines of the gag I began to cough, as quietly as I could, to attract his attention.

'What do you want?' He sounded annoyed but it was too late now. He pulled down my gag.

'I'm sorry, I need to use the loo. I'm desperate,' I added, not entirely for effect.

He tutted extravagantly. 'I'm not having this every day. I told you what the toilet arrangements were – once in the morning and once at night.'

'I'm sorry.'

'You'll go back in the box if you carry on like this,' he warned, as he lifted the blanket off me and guided me to the bucket. I shuffled along beside him trying to apologise through the gag.

'I'm sorry, I won't do it again,' I mumbled.

'No, well, see that you don't.'

Christ, I thought, as I sat on the bucket, please don't say that I've messed things up already. Lying on the mattress for hours was bad enough, but the thought of being stuck in that box all day and then all night was too horrible to contemplate.

'I'm really sorry,' I repeated as he helped me back to the mattress.

'Your mouth's dribbling,' he said roughly, handing me a piece of toilet paper. 'You can take the gag out if you want. But I don't have to warn you what will happen if you make a sound, do I?'

He removed the tape and the soggy rolled-up gag that was wedged in my mouth. It was wonderful to be rid of that foul rag.

The radio, tuned to Radio Two, played all the time. I had never listened to it before – most of the music seemed to be from the fifties or the early sixties, a bit before my time – but Bob seemed to enjoy it: he hummed or sang along to a lot of the tunes. I only really pricked up my ears when I heard the pre-news jingle. I wondered if there would be anything on about me, but after listening to several bulletins I dismissed the idea. They were talking about world politics and aircraft disasters; it seemed hardly likely that Stephanie Slater disappearing in Birmingham would warrant a mention.

Lying on the mattress under a blanket my tortured back was beginning to return to normal, although my arms continued to throb well into the following day.

·5·

BOB CAME IN a couple of times to give me bits of chocolate and at one point to tell me he was taking the dog out for a walk.

'What sort of a dog is it?' I asked him, regretting the question the second it was out of my mouth. I hoped he wouldn't think I was trying to trick him or trip him up. In general, making conversation, I had decided, would be a good thing, because it would help the process of him beginning to see me as another human being, but I didn't want him to think I was playing detective. I didn't want to know anything about him if it was going to rebound on me later. Fortunately, he seemed to think it was a normal question to ask.

'It's an Alsatian, a six-month-old bitch.'

'I like dogs,' I said, trying to keep up the momentum. 'Well, I like all animals really. I have two cats at home.'

'You wouldn't like this one,' he said curtly. 'It won't do anything it's told. Disobedient, or daft, I don't know which.'

'They all have their personalities, don't they?' I said, trying to lighten the conversation. I wasn't a bit surprised that the dog was daft. He had done nothing but shout and throw things at it since he'd brought it in – it was probably scared to death of him.

Before he took the dog out he placed the toilet roll on my right shoulder, positioning a few loose sheets in a certain way.

'Right, remember what I told you about keeping quiet and don't move either. I'll only be just outside the door with the dog, but I have left this in a special way and if you move I'll know.'

I heard him leave the building but felt sure he must have crept back. I was convinced that he was testing me. He had left me alone without the gag and with only a leg manacle on to see what I would do. I knew it was impossible to escape but even so the temptation to get up and try to feel my way around was overwhelming. I also wanted to reach down and check out the leg iron, but the thought of the toilet roll carefully positioned on my shoulder and the certainty that somewhere he was watching me prevented me from doing any of these things. Ten minutes or so later he returned, checked the toilet roll and seemed satisfied because he removed it without a word.

I lay on the mattress and for what must have been the four-hundredth time reran in my mind the events that had brought me to this place. Could I have been more cautious at Turnberry Road? Should I have taken the opportunity to attract someone's attention as Bob walked me down the garden of the house? No, I told myself, you were blindfolded and gagged, your hands and feet were tied, and he had a knife pressed up against your body. You couldn't have done anything. But the niggling doubts remained. I'm not a hysterical sort of person; I tend not to get over-excited about things. One of the reasons I enjoy driving is because, unlike most of my friends, I rarely get upset by other road users. If somebody behind me is in a desperate rush to overtake I would rather pull over and let them than have flashing lights in my mirror and a lot of bad feeling. Maybe that same laid-back attitude had allowed Bob to get away with this. I was unable to shake off the thought that I might have missed a chance somewhere along the line.

I heard the sound of the metal door being dragged across its metal runner at about five o'clock. Not long after that Bob appeared in the back of the workshop.

'What do you want for your tea?' he asked.

'Chips,' I said. It was the first thing that came into my head, and in any case I didn't have the impression that the place was fitted out with too many mod cons. That morning, while he was making the tea, I recalled him mentioning that there wasn't even running water. He was recounting some tale about filling the kettle with cleaning fluid by mistake and having a difficult job cleaning it out, but I had been in too much pain to pay him any attention then. From now on, I would have to be looking out for conversation opportunities.

'Right, we'll have chips again tonight and tomorrow I'll sort out some proper food,' he promised. 'I'll have to go and get them but I'm leaving the dog here to guard you. I'm not going to make you put the gag back in, but I don't want you to make a sound. I'm going to trust you on this, but I'm warning you, don't let me down.'

'I won't, I promise.' I heard a car drive away and for the fifteen minutes or so he was away I lay wondering if this was another elaborate test. Apparently it wasn't, because following the sound of a car drawing up outside, he reappeared with the chips. He didn't eat, but watched me as I fumbled in the open packet. He was in a mood to talk.

'So, Stephanie Slater, tell me about yourself. I can't tell you about me, but we can talk about you.'

'There's not that much to tell, really. I was born in 1966 and I've lived with my Mum and Dad in Great Barr, in the same house actually, all my life.'

'Have you got a boyfriend?'

'Yes, I have – David.'

'And is it serious?'

'No, not really. He has to work late quite a bit so we don't get the chance to go out much, but he's a good laugh – we get on well.'

'Have you never thought of getting married?'

'Not seriously,' I laughed. 'I probably haven't met the right person yet. I've nothing against marriage, though. I might do it one day – who knows? Most people seem to. But I'm not in any hurry.'

'You do right,' he responded in his northern accent.

'I know my Mum and Dad would like to see me married, well, my Mum especially. She can't wait to see me in the big white dress, and then there's the grandchildren, of course. I think that's what she would really like, grandchildren.' I nattered on nineteen to the dozen and it wasn't solely for the purpose of establishing a rapport: I realised how much I had missed the sound of another voice in conversation. All day I had lain on the mattress where I now sat, having conversations with myself. It was nice to hear the sound of another voice apart from the radio, even if it was his.

'Too many folk marry young. There wouldn't be all this divorce if they waited for a bit. I don't agree with it myself, getting married young and then getting divorced. It's very hard on the children, too, when their parents split up. Eat your chips.'

'They're still a bit hot,' I said, nibbling at the edge of one.

'Are your Mum and Dad happy?'

'Oh yes, very. I'm adopted, actually.'

'Oh no, don't say that!' He sounded distressed, as if I had said something that would make him feel worse than he already did. I was quite taken aback.

'It's all right,' I reassured him. 'I have a smashing Mum and Dad, they are lovely. I had a very happy childhood and we are still really close.' Still there was silence from Bob. I blundered on.

'They couldn't have children, so they adopted me when I was six months old.'

'I would have liked children,' he said, but since he didn't elaborate, neither did I, sensing that the topic might have fallen under the heading of 'information best not known'.

We continued to chat about my job, how much I was paid and how commission on the sale of a house was allocated. He asked me if I had enjoyed school and told me that he had left with good grades.

'What do you do for a social life, then, if your boyfriend works late?' he asked me at one point.

I was into my stride by this time, feeling pleased with myself for having established an exchange with this pre-viously taciturn character. 'I have quite a lot of friends as well as David, and usually a group of us meet up in the Malt Shovel – that's my local pub – for a few drinks and a laugh.'

'I don't go into pubs,' he replied sourly.

Whoops, had I made a gaffe saying that? Perhaps he was teetotal; I didn't want him thinking I was some kind of lush.

'Not every night, of course,' I quickly chipped in. 'Most evenings one or two of my friends come over to my house and we sit in my room talking and listening to music. The pub is more of a weekend meeting place, really.'

'I never go into them – that's how people get caught.'

'What do you mean?'

'When people do something, you know, like when they

steal a car or break into a shop or something, then they go into the pub and sit drinking with their mates, bragging about what they have done. The drink loosens their tongue – they start shouting their mouth off for everyone to hear and then they're surprised when they get a call from the police. It's stupid. My mate goes in pubs a lot.'

'Your mate?' It was probably best not to know but the question was out before I had considered it.

'The bloke I'm doing this with – you know, keeping you.'

'Oh.' So there *was* more than one of them.

'You're lucky you didn't get him; he's a nasty piece of work, I can tell you.'

'What do you mean?'

'He's not the sort of person you would want to have looking after you. He's the sort of chap who would rather give you a bunch of fives than a bag of chips.' He sniggered. 'He's a rough 'un, all right, you're lucky, you take my word for it.'

I didn't know what to say. The thought of anybody else being involved was bad enough but if Bob, this man who had attacked me, cut me, raped me and the rest, thought his mate was a bad lot, he must be a bloody psychopath.

'Have you finished those chips?' he asked, businesslike once more.

'Yes, I don't want any more, thanks, I wasn't very hungry.'

'Right, then, I think it's time you went back in the box.'

There was no point making a big fuss. If that's where he had decided to put me, that's where I knew I would end up, although the thought filled me with dread.

'Not the box?' I asked hopefully.

'I'm afraid so. Now, do you need to use the toilet before

you settle down for the night? There's an extra cardigan here if you want it, in case you're cold.'

As I eased my way back into the box I realised that he had done some work on it. That must have been what he had been doing with the electric saw that afternoon. The wooden coffin which the previous night had caused me so much pain had been cut down and now reached from my neck to the top of my thighs rather than right down to enclose my feet. This meant I could lie flat on my back with just the top part of my body in the coffin, with the rest of me encased only by the plastic bin. Where he had sawn the wood it was rough and scratchy, but I could handle that, especially since he had now provided a duvet for me to wrap myself in, in addition to the blanket.

'Is that better?' he asked.

'It's much better – thanks a lot, it's made a big difference.' I didn't attempt to keep the gratitude out of my voice. All day I had been dreading the moment when I would be forced to return to the box; the thought of the pain and the cold of last night had been almost enough to make me take a chance and call out to one of those disembodied voices I had heard talking to Bob in the front part of the workshop. I was glad now I hadn't. The sleeping arrangements were still nobody's idea of comfort, but after what I had endured the previous night the box felt almost luxurious to me.

I still experienced a momentary panic as I heard him slide the bolt into place and roll a large stone or boulder in front of the lid but I managed to get myself under control almost immediately. All day long, while I had been lying quietly on the mattress as well as when I had been trying to keep conversations going with Bob, I had been aware that beneath my calm exterior a geyser of raw emotion was desperate to blow. I must not let that happen. I must not crack up, I had repeated to myself. I instinctively knew that the only way I would get out of that place alive would be to play it cool. Whatever happened I must always keep that right at the front of my mind.

The sound of his car had long died away; the only noises now were of birds or rats scuffling about in the darkness above my head. There must be an upstairs or an attic, I thought. Bob had certainly given me plenty to think about.

I felt I had made some progress in getting him to see me as another human being rather than as an object. The fact that he had modified the coffin must be a good sign. If he intended to kill me, would he take the time and trouble? It didn't seem likely, but the thought of death was never out of my mind for very long. However relaxed I tried to appear when with him, I was always aware of the danger. I was very glad I had not attempted to call out when I heard voices in the workshop or disturbed the toilet roll he had left on my shoulder when he took the dog out. I seemed to have passed his stupid tests but thank God I had, if it meant I wouldn't have to keep that hateful gag in my mouth all day or wear handcuffs on my hands and legs. There probably wasn't any chance of getting him to remove the blindfold – obviously he wouldn't want me to see him – but on the whole, I felt that I had made considerable progress.

I didn't like the sound of his mate, and the thought that he might appear at the workshop frightened me. From what Bob said it seemed that there were just the two of them involved. Perhaps the mate was the brains behind the scheme and Bob was just, as he had described himself, the babysitter. Maybe the mate had come up with the idea of a kidnap and Bob had been roped in to do the dirty work of snatching someone and providing the premises. The workshop was clearly an established business. The two of them hadn't rented an old barn in the country for the express purpose of holding me hostage.

Even though Bob had described his mate as a nasty piece of work, his voice had sounded strangely admiring when he spoke about him, almost like a little boy talking about his older brother – 'he's horrible and I hate him but he's ever so good at football and the fastest runner in the school'. It worried me because I knew what Bob was capable of on his own account. I remembered the feeling of dread when I heard the metal door grate closed and Bob came to ask me what I wanted for tea. It had been after giving me the chips the night before that he had raped me. But I didn't want to think about that any more. If I was going to get through this, I must push all thoughts of that right out of my mind; if every time he spoke I heard only the voice of a rapist, I was lost. He had said I would not be killed, that I would be going home, and I must believe that. I must.

The next morning I awoke to the sound of a motor bike being revved up in the front part of the workshop. The box seemed to be filling up with fumes. In spite of all my positive thinking I immediately felt sure that this was how Bob had decided to kill me – by carbon monoxide poisoning. Then the revving stopped, but I could hear the engine continuing to tick over. I pulled the duvet up over my face. I had read newspaper accounts of people killing themselves in cars by running a hose from the exhaust to the inside. The whole place would eventually fill up with noxious fumes and I would die, here in this coffin. The bastard, and after all he had said. I pushed my face deeper into the quilt. As I struggled to push the pillow against the lid of the bin in the hope of preventing more fumes from entering it, I heard the metal door grate open and the motor bike move off. I lay still for a minute listening to the noise of its engine fading into the distance before pulling down the duvet. The air in the box was thick with fumes. I had over-reacted, I knew, but for those few minutes I had been absolutely convinced I was about to be gassed.

Somewhere in the workshop the radio sprang to life but almost immediately the volume decreased and I heard footsteps approaching the door.

'Did you hear that?' It was Bob.

'The motor bike? Yes.'

'That were my mate.'

I didn't need to ask if it was the same mate. His tone of voice told me that it was.

'Yes, he came to collect his bike. He will be needing that to pick up the money.'

'Oh.' I would have liked to have said more but the thought that his mate had actually been here, in the building, was a horrible one. Thank God he hadn't stayed around.

'Have you got your blindfold on?'

With my hands free of the handcuffs I had managed to remove it during the night but it was back in place now.

'Yes, it's on.'

The lid of the bin swung open and again I had a sense of profound relief. This morning I felt stiff and cold after spending the night in the box but not numb and frozen as I had the previous day. Bob helped me out of the box and on to the hard-backed chair. He had already switched on the electric heater which was placed close to the chair. I tried to position my icy cold feet in front of the heat. The fumes from the motor-bike exhaust still hung heavy in the air.

Bob laughed as I wrinkled up my nose.

'Aye, it stinks a bit, doesn't it?'

'It does,' I agreed. 'It gave me the shock of my life when

I woke up to that – I thought you were trying to gas me or something.'

Now why had I said that? I was astonished with myself. I was supposed to be playing it cool, very relaxed and laid back, and the minute he gets me out of the box I'm whining.

I couldn't understand it that morning, but now I do. I was quite simply desperate for reassurance. I had resolved to be strong and to push the bad thoughts, those that concentrated on his violence or my fears, out of my mind. While I could do this fairly successfully at one level by simply crowding out a thought that was too painful with another thought, at a deeper level this process didn't work. All the time I was trying to keep the bad thoughts from the forefront of my mind, they were churning away just beneath the surface. I couldn't solve them so I didn't want to address them, but neither could I make them go away. So the minute that Bob acknowledged the motor-bike fumes my fear that he was going to kill me, a bad thought, crashed through the barrier I had erected.

I thought my panicky admission might annoy him but when he spoke it was in a quiet, measured way. 'I've told you, I'm not going to kill you. You're going home when this is sorted out, back to your Mum and Dad. My mate wanted to come in and have a look at you but I told him to leave you alone. Don't worry, I'll look after you.'

The kindliness of his tone made me more vulnerable than if he had shouted. I felt quite tearful, but tried to keep the catch out of my voice as I reached out my hand. After only a moment's hesitation he took it in both of his.

'I am going home, aren't I? Please tell me that I am.'

'Yes, you are going home, Stephanie, I promise.'

*   *   *

As he bustled about the workshop preparing porridge and tea he chatted to me, but I was preoccupied with thoughts of the exchange that had just taken place. My reaching for his hand had not been contrived but born out of genuine desperation that he may not have had any intention of ever allowing me to return to my real life.

'When you've had your breakfast I'll get you some water organised to have a bit of a wash. I've brought you a change of pants, a pair of my own Y-fronts, but they'll have to do.'

'Do you think I could brush my hair as well?' I asked. My hair, which was waist-length and quite thick, was in a terrible state. Since the night I had arrived there and Bob had removed the bobble that kept it off my face, it seemed to have adopted a life of its own, falling over my face or getting caught up behind my head in the box.

'Yes, I've brought a hairbrush as well, so you can get properly spruced up. You can take your blindfold off to have a wash and that but keep your eyes closed, do you understand?'

'Yes.'

'And when you've finished I've a fresh blindfold for you.'

After I'd eaten a bowl of lumpy porridge and drunk a mug of sweet, strong tea, Bob produced a rectangular plastic bowl of hot water and placed it on my lap.

'Right, here's a bar of soap,' he said, putting it into my hand, 'and here's a towel. Do you want a flannel?'

'No, thanks, I can manage.'

The hot water felt wonderful. It was my first wash in more than forty-eight hours and I certainly needed it. The palm of my hand, where Bob's knife had sliced into it, was stiff and sore again now I had washed the dried blood from it. I hadn't realised he was watching me until he said, 'I'll get you some Germolene to rub on that.'

As he took the bowl from my lap and walked away I attempted to clean my teeth with a corner of the hard, rough towel he had given me.

'I never thought about a toothbrush – I'll bring you one in tomorrow.'

'Thanks,' I muttered.

Did he never stop watching me, I wondered to myself? I had been aware of him staring at me when I'd used the makeshift loo that morning. He'd been right when he told me to forget any sense of modesty I may have had, on the day he kidnapped me. I still found it embarrassing and uncomfortable though, being forced to use the loo while being watched, and I dreaded the thought of having to change my underwear in front of him. Last time he had made me get undressed . . . No, I wasn't going down that road again.

As I brushed my hair I started to talk to him in a chatty sort of way. I discovered he was a fan of the television programme *Coronation Street*, which is also a favourite of mine. My parents have always watched it and although I lost interest for a while when I was in my teens, for years I had rarely missed it. It was also exactly the sort of conversation I wanted to be having as I changed my knickers. He stood beside me as I took off my boots, the jeans he had given me, and my knickers, and then put on the clean underwear he gave me. One of the serial's recent storylines had concerned the death of a baby born prematurely.

'Wasn't it sad when Liz McDonald lost the baby?'

'Yeah, it was. She's a good actress that plays Liz, isn't she?'

'They all are, aren't they? I think it's really good, really believable. I never miss it – I won't go out until it's been on, or else I video it.'

'I watched it on the video on Wednesday.'

I'll bet you did, you bastard, the thought crowded into

71

my head. You couldn't have been raping me in this God-forsaken place and watching *Coronation Street* at the same time, could you? But I managed to bite it back. Instead I gave a little laugh and said, 'Oh, did you? What happened?'

As he outlined the events that had taken place, I got back into my clothes.

When I was dressed he asked me if my feet were warm enough. I told him they were cold, and he put an extra pair of socks over the first pair.

'They are cold, aren't they?' he said, feeling my feet with one hand as he pulled the socks up with the other. 'I'll get you a pair of them moon boots, they're supposed to be warm, aren't they?'

While Bob was capable of behaving in a very caring way, there was another side to him that seemed to enjoy seeing me frightened. As I was sitting on the hard-backed chair he was fiddling about inside the box, straightening the blanket and sorting out the duvet. The previous night I had felt what I imagined to be rags at the bottom of the box. Bob appeared to have just come across them. 'Well, look at these!' he said, in a voice of mock disgust.

Obviously I couldn't, since he had covered my eyes with the new blindfold, a superior version which seemed to be made up of thick crepe material and secured with three elasticated strings at the back.

'What is it?' I asked.

'My God, just look at these!' he repeated.

Did he mean it? Did he want me to take the blindfold off and look at whatever it was that had so surprised him?

'What is it?' I said again.

'It's underwear, knickers and bras and God knows what, if you can call them knickers and bras, what there is of them.'

'Oh, how did they get there?' I didn't really want to be

involved in this conversation but didn't know how to respond.

'They must be my mate's. Yes, he must have got these from somewhere, or someone!' He laughed raucously.

I began to feel very uncomfortable. Why would anybody put what, from the tone of Bob's voice, was clearly kinky underwear in the bottom of a plastic bin? Where would he have got them from and why? Christ, the horrible thought occurred to me, I hope he didn't get them for me. I felt a sudden chill. Oh no, they couldn't be planning to make me do that. Behind me, over at the bin, Bob was still marvelling at the decadence of his mate, in that same hero-worshipping tone of voice. He was giving me the creeps. I said nothing, but the damage had been done, just as he intended it should. He knew I was scared stiff at the very thought of his mate; there was no need to go to such lengths to make him sound like a pervert as well as a sadist.

Over the days there would be many demonstrations of the double-sidedness of Bob's personality. For instance when he put me back in the box after breakfast he had fixed up a switch which he said I could use to attract his attention when he was in the other part of the workshop. If I pressed the switch a light would flash and he would know I needed him. However, I balanced this act of kindness against a horribly distressing conversation that followed shortly after his 'discovery' of the kinky underwear. 'I'll have to get rid of that bin now,' he announced.

'Which bin is that?' I said keenly, always anxious to get the conversation between us flowing.

'There's a plastic wheely bin in the corner over there. I was going to wheel your body out in it.'

·6·

I WAS CRUSHED. Foolishly, when he'd talked of getting rid of the bin, I'd imagined he was referring to the plastic bin I had been forced to sleep in. After all, I seemed to have passed all his little tests and yesterday, after he had allowed me to remain on the mattress without gag or handcuffs, I had proved I was trustworthy by not calling out. Last night, and again this morning, we had been chatting together quite happily, and I really felt progress had been made. Now it seemed that all the time I had spent in the workshop, all those tedious, awful hours, had been spent in the same room as the bin he had intended to use to get rid of my body.

'My body?' I croaked.

'Yes, we planned to wheel you out in that plastic bin and then get rid of the body.' He sniggered. 'I nearly had a fit when I saw you at the house. My heart sank and I said to myself, "Oh no, she's too big – she'll never fit into that bin." But it doesn't matter now, because we won't be needing it, will we?'

'You aren't going to kill me, are you, Bob?'

'No, I've just told you, haven't I? I'm going to get rid

of the bin I was going to use to dump you. Of course I'm not going to kill you!'

'And you won't let your mate come here again?'

'Well, I can't promise that. He calls in now and again if he's in the area – we don't make appointments.'

'I really don't want him to come, Bob. You won't let him kill me, will you?'

'Of course he won't kill you.'

'Promise, Bob, promise you won't let him hurt me.'

'I promise – there will be no hurting and no killing. You'll be going home when all this is over.'

'Will I? I really want to go home. I really want to see my Mum and Dad and I'm scared that I might never see them again.'

'Now that's enough,' he said, though not unkindly, 'I've told you that you're going home and you are. Right, come on, I've a lot on my plate today so I want you back in the box.'

He had cut a number of circular air holes about an inch and a half in diameter, along the length of the plastic bin so that if the workshop light was on, a little filtered in, even when the lid was closed. On being returned to the box I had pulled the new elasticated blindfold up over my eyes. I lay in the semi-darkness thinking about what Bob had said and why he had said it. Had he really intended to allay my fear of being murdered by telling me he now intended to get rid of the bin that had been intended to remove my body? Until a minute earlier he had never admitted that killing me had ever been a consideration. He had warned that although he and his mate didn't want to hurt me they would do so 'if they had to', but right from the morning he had kidnapped me in Turnberry Road, Bob had seemed almost at pains to reassure me that if I behaved myself I would be released as soon as the ransom was paid. Now I didn't know what to believe.

I remained in the box for most of the day. I didn't know whether I was being punished for wanting to use the lavatory yesterday or whether Bob had to go out somewhere and didn't want to leave me on the mattress. I couldn't always tell whether he was in the building or not. Obviously, if I heard the grating of the metal door and then the sound of a car driving away I assumed he had gone out, then I would lie waiting and listening for his return. Generally, I felt, he told me if he was going away for some time but I didn't really know. There was always the radio in the background. It was set to come on at 8 am and it went off again in the early hours of the following morning. Radio Two would never have been my choice but I was often glad of the sound of another human voice, particularly at night after Bob had gone. However, to hear an announcement at ten o'clock in the morning about what programme would be coming on at ten o'clock that night could be a soul-destroying experience. I will be here for that, I reminded myself. Twelve hours from now I will still be here in this box when that programme comes on. And I'll be here two hours later when it finishes, I am going nowhere.

By the time Bob took me out of the box for something to eat in the evening I had had hours to consider my position. I felt all the talk about the bin to remove my body had been intended to frighten rather than reassure me. There had been no need to mention the bin at all. He knew I hadn't seen it, I hadn't the faintest idea it was there so his motives could only have been to keep me on my toes. He didn't want me to become complaisant. We could chat together, in fact I felt he was beginning to enjoy our conversations but perhaps he also thought I was forgetting who was in charge. Not that I did forget, not for a second. I tried very hard with Bob, to talk and even to laugh with him. From day one my primary objective had been to persuade him of my existence as a human being, rather than an object. But despite conversations that might have sounded almost light-hearted, I never – not ever – felt less than terrified about what he might do to me. I was set on a survival course and quite prepared to play whatever role was required to get me out of the place alive.

Although I believed he had talked about the bin to frighten me, I didn't doubt he was telling the truth about his original intention to use it to dump my body. If that was the case it meant something had changed his mind, something had made him decide to let me live, either that or he was quite simply lying through his teeth and he would kill me when it was over anyway. One part of me was saying, 'Don't believe him, don't believe him. Look what he's done already, he's a madman,' while another voice was insisting: 'Believe him, you have to believe him or you will fall apart and then you're done for.' I wasn't ready yet to resign myself to dying. I decided to keep up the campaign to win his regard. I had no choice.

I was stiff when he got me out of the box for tea. He held on to my hands and told me to bend my knees a few times and do some running on the spot.

'You'll soon stiffen up if you don't do a bit of exercise,' he noted, adding that he had been very athletic as a lad. You wouldn't be so supple yourself if you had spent the number of hours in that box I have, I thought as I jogged about on the spot. For tea that evening he offered me a selection of soups, tomato, vegetable or chicken. I chose tomato: I could hear him opening the tin and as he did so complaining that I wasn't eating enough.

'I should organise some proper food for you really, some vegetables and stuff. I grow my own vegetables,' he threw in almost as an afterthought.

'Do you?' I asked, ever alert to a conversational opening.

'Yes, I live out in the country, it's quite a big house,

detached you know. It must be worth about £100,000 and I've got a nice big greenhouse as well.'

'That must be nice – it's a nice way to pass the time, gardening.'

'Well there's not much happens this time of year, of course. It'll be a few weeks yet before the ground's ready for working.'

'I expect you get a bit fed up in the winter months.' Maybe that's why you decided to kidnap me in the dead of winter, I thought bitterly, because there wasn't enough to keep you busy in the greenhouse.

'No, I've a lot of other interests beside gardening. I'm doing a lot of work on a new computer I've just bought, at the moment.'

'Oh!' I suspect my voice registered surprise. I didn't think Bob was the computer type somehow.

'Are you writing a book or something?' I went on.

'No.' I could hear the smile in his voice. 'No, it's nowt like that. I'm inputting a lot of information, for the business and that. Well, I'm trying to input a lot of information, I should say, I spent hours at it one night, then when I went back to it in the morning, it had all disappeared. There were nothing on it at all. Hours of work down the drain. I was really annoyed, got on to the manufacturers and everything. They told me to send the disc back to them, which I did but even when it came back it still didn't work.'

'Oh dear, that's a bit of a problem isn't it?'

'No, it seems to be sorted out now. I think I've got the hang of it.'

'What was wrong then?' I couldn't have cared less about his stupid computer but I would have happily conversed about the estimated life expectancy of a dandelion clock if he had expressed any interest in the subject.

'Oh, it were my fault. I wasn't doing something I should

have to save the information in the memory bank. I didn't read the instructions properly so every time I turned the machine off, all the information disappeared. I finally managed to sort it out but only after a bit of a set-to with the manufacturers.'

'I believe computers can be very complicated. I haven't had much to do with them, to be honest. I tried to write a book a couple of years ago and just about everybody told me I ought to get a computer to do it. In the end I believed that if I got a computer the book would write itself.'

'Well I should think they would be ideal for that because you can add bits in, take bits out, even shift bits around – and there's no crossing out or mess when you've finished. You just print it up and it's all laid out like typing, just the job for book writing I'd say.'

'I managed without one, although maybe that's why I didn't manage to get it published,' I said with a laugh.

'What was it about then, this book?'

'It was basically a story about a highwayman called Master Jack.' I went on to outline the plot of the story I had written and how I had sent it off to a publisher in Devon who said they would publish it if I paid them two thousand pounds. 'I think it might have been a bit of a fiddle,' I concluded.

Bob was an attentive listener: I got the impression he was genuinely interested in what I had to say. I have always been a chatty sort of person. Teachers at school would tell Mum and Dad that I would get through life okay, if not on brains then on personality. Once I was into my flow it wasn't difficult to keep conversation going, although I was always careful to steer clear of any subjects I thought might compromise him. Occasionally, he would reveal something about himself during our talks, for example when he described something personal, such as his interests, he would mutter, 'I shouldn't have said that, should I?'

At such times I would do my best to reassure him. 'Don't worry,' I would say, almost conspiratorially, 'I didn't hear that, I won't say anything.'

I can't honestly say what was in my mind when I gave him those reassurances; I just wanted to get on with him during the time I was there and to get out in one piece at the end of it.

That night, after he left saying, as he always did, 'Good-night then, see you in the morning,' I lay in the box wondering about the events of the day as Radio Two droned in the background. During the day I had heard him sawing again and before leaving that evening he confirmed that the bin intended to remove my body had been destroyed. I was immensely relieved although far from reassured.

I wondered about Mum and Dad. My mother had always suffered with what we called 'her nerves'. Often upset and anxious when under pressure, I dreaded to think what this must be doing to her. She and Dad adopted me when I was just six months old. My birth mother was unmarried and unable to afford to keep me, and I grew up knowing I had been adopted and all the circumstances involved. Friends have asked if it feels different. It doesn't to me because it's the only life I have known.

When I was seventeen I managed to trace my birth mother, without Mum and Dad's knowledge. After a number of telephone calls I arranged to meet up with her outside the Odeon cinema in Birmingham. She was with the man who is now her husband, not my natural father, and they have children of their own. She seemed too young to be my Mum but the meeting was a success: we went for a coffee and had a long talk. She told me about my natural father who is also now married with a family.

Later I even went to her home and met her children. She seemed like a nice woman and I liked her, but I can't say the meeting changed my life as I probably hoped it would.

Seventeen is a funny age: no longer a schoolgirl, I was developing and changing in lots of ways. Mum especially found the emerging personality a bit difficult to cope with. Looking back on it I might have been a bit over the top. I followed a style the kids then called Gothic. It was stunning really: black frock coats and white shirts frilled at the neck. I loved it but my Mum thought it was just weird. She would have preferred to see me in a polyester two-piece suit in a nice shade of apricot, 'to bring out the colour of your skin'. She firmly believes that the most rewarding role in life a woman can have is to be a good wife and mother and while I don't necessarily disagree with that, I knew it wasn't for me, certainly not at seventeen.

I didn't set out to find my birth mother with the intention of dumping my adoptive Mum but I know I wondered if I might have inherited some of what Mum and Dad might have described then as my 'weird ways' from the woman who carried me for nine months.

When I met her outside the Odeon, I realised that in her own way she was just as ordinary as my Mum at home and as ordinary as everybody else's Mum, come to that. Now it seems obvious that she would be, but at seventeen it wasn't. We saw each other twice and we have kept in touch, albeit in a fairly haphazard way – we don't talk or write to each other on a regular basis. So when I lay in the box thinking of Mum and Dad there was no ambiguity: it was Betty and Warren Slater I wondered and worried about, the two people who despite our rows and disagreements over the years had always been there for me, offering love and support.

I thought too about my friends. Tonight was Friday. Normally, I would have watched *Red Dwarf*, my absolute favourite television programme, and then been on my way to the Malt Shovel by now. A group of us met up there regularly on a Friday, for a drink and a laugh. I had known most of the people for years, mostly since schooldays. I wondered if they had been told anything. They would think it very strange if I just didn't turn up and I wondered particularly about Lisa, my best friend. She and I saw each other virtually every evening: what would she be doing? Thinking about home made me feel very down. I tried to snap myself out of it by running through the entire script of an episode of *Red Dwarf* that I have watched at least two dozen times on video.

The cold intensified as the hours dragged by. Although Bob had given me extra clothes to wear and bedding to wrap myself in, I was always freezing and uncomfortable during the night. I longed to be able to pull my knees up and snuggle down into my own bed at home. Instead, I lay the most comfortable way I could in the restricted space of the box and waited for morning.

The days followed a pattern now. Bob would get me out of the box, give me porridge and tea for breakfast, provide me with water in which to wash, and hold my hands while I did a couple of minutes' running on the spot. True to his word, on Saturday morning he arrived with a toothbrush, moon boots to keep my feet warm and Germolene to put on the knife wound on my hand and my elbow, which was sore from lying in the box. He asked me if I had any bed sores. If so he could help, he said: he had picked up a few tips from his girlfriend, who used to be a nurse. I didn't really know what bed sores were but I felt fairly confident I didn't have any, so I thanked him and said it was okay.

Again he took me to task, reminding me I had nothing to thank him for. He had snapped at me four or five times for the same thing but saying thank you was an automatic thing for me and anyway, I wanted him to recognise that despite everything he had done I was treating him civilly and hoped it would inspire him to do the same.

'Right, let's get these moon boots on, shall we? Are your feet still cold?' he asked.

My feet were so cold I could barely feel them. I was aware that sometimes I hobbled rather than walked because of the numbness in them. As he eased off my own black leather boots I winced. I had been wearing them for four days and three nights, and they felt as if they were moulded to my feet. Bob held a foot in each hand.

'I think we had better bathe these,' he said, his voice full of concern, 'they are very cold. But I will have to have your permission, I don't want you charging me with assault.'

Assault? Assault? Was the man completely out of his mind, was he aware of what was going on here? I had been kidnapped, knifed and raped by him, and here he was asking permission to bathe my feet in case I charged him with assault.

'Permission granted,' I said, with a wave of my hand and what I hoped was a regal nod. I could be as crazy as him if that's what it took. He boiled a kettle and after preparing a bowl full of wonderfully warm water, tenderly helped restore a sense of feeling to my icy cold feet.

For some reason Saturday didn't seem to be as busy as the other days had been: hardly anyone came into the other part of the workshop and he seemed quite happy to sit about and chat. We talked about many things. He asked me if I was expecting to have a period, assuring me that if I was he would make some arrangements, but I told him it wasn't necessary. We spoke of astronomy, which is one of my hobbies, and from what he said it was clear that he had some knowledge of star constellations. He referred to Cassiopeia, the Great Bear, the Little Bear and

Orion. I told him that at school I had been interested in history, how I had always had a soft spot for highwaymen and especially admired Dick Turpin – I had called one of my cats Swift Nick after another legendary highwayman. The idea seemed to amuse him.

I also mentioned the Titanic disaster, which has always fascinated me, but he wasn't really interested in that so I dropped it in favour of a discussion on other forms of travel. Bob said that if he had to travel any distance he travelled by train, and he told me about seeing the astronomer Patrick Moore during one journey and the two actresses from the television series *Birds of a Feather* during another.

I have never been what you would call a great traveller. When I was young family holidays were always spent on the Isle of Wight. I remember the excitement of leaving Great Barr in July, the car packed high with suitcases and travel bags, for our two weeks on the island. I have always loved the place, its beauty and serenity. Even when I was a child it seemed to belong to a past era, a time when people weren't too busy to pass the time of day or stop to offer an opinion on the best way to get from Ryde to Ventnor.

I told Bob about the island and how I loved it. He had never been there but could well see the attraction of leaving the hurly-burly of Birmingham for a fortnight to stay somewhere like that. He told me he had done a lot of travelling at one time. He mentioned being in Egypt and seeing the pyramids. While I thought Egypt must be a fascinating place, I told him I didn't think I would get on very well with the intense heat there. I went to Spain once and thought I would explode, it was so hot. Bob laughed at that and said he liked to lie in the sun and relax whilst on holiday.

These exchanges were made over the course of a few

hours as I sat in the hard-backed chair and he pottered about doing things in different areas of the workshop. He also discussed plans for my release. There were various options, he said. He could drop me off at a telephone box, where I could first of all phone the police and then my parents. An alternative would be for him to leave me within a hundred yards of a police station or a hospital somewhere in the Uttoxeter area. From the way he spoke I felt he was still mulling over the possibilities. He didn't seem to be inviting suggestions from me so I didn't make any. But just the thought of being left alone in a telephone box or free to walk into a police station or hospital filled me with elation. To pull off the blindfold, to be able to shout and wave my arms in the air, to go where I wanted and most of all to be able to see where I was – the very idea made me feel giddy.

At around two o'clock Bob asked me if I would like a mug of soup. This time I chose vegetable. I thought perhaps he had decided to throw lunch in as well today since it was the weekend. What I didn't realise was that he would be closing up the workshop at three o'clock and going home.

When he had gone I had time to contemplate all that had happened. We had covered a lot of ground that morning and as a result I felt I had a much better understanding of what made him tick. He was clearly a bright chap who had done a few things in his life and maintained a variety of interests. In spite of that, from the odd throwaway comment about his mate, I got the impression Bob was not the brains behind my kidnap – more the organ grinder's monkey than the organ grinder. When he talked of his mate he always sounded in awe of him. Despite his apparent disapproval of his mate's drinking, womanising and general 'hard man' attitude, there was an unmistakable tone of admiration in his voice whenever he referred to him.

I wondered again what sort of man this mate must be and prayed I would never have to meet him face to face.

By this time I knew better than to allow thoughts of home, Mum and Dad or my friends, into the box with me. They made me too unhappy and I was already teetering on an emotional tightrope. I knew it was not yet half-past three in the afternoon, which meant Bob would not be back for at least seventeen hours. He had given me two small bars of chocolate and a pint of milk as well as a sort of plastic seed tray which he said I should use as a loo in an emergency. It wasn't the thought of hunger or thirst or needing the loo that bothered me but those endless hours of solitary inactivity stretching before me. I knew for certain that if I acknowledged how I felt, if I allowed the thought that I was going to be banged up in the box for seventeen hours to come to the surface of my mind, I was done for. To do that would be to face the prospect of filling that time, knowing there was no way I could do it. I knew that the only way was to take it minute by minute. I may have been inside the box but my mind could leave it at will. When the radio went off at 1 am, I was still wide awake.

I had enjoyed reciting the script of a half-hour episode of *Red Dwarf* to myself the day before and went through my mind for other possibilities. Before long I was well into it, the episode where Rimmer meets the only other hologram in existence but then discovers that she isn't. I was speaking all the parts, using the same intonations I had heard so many times on the video. At one point I realised I was even tittering to myself as I acted out a particularly funny scene between Rimmer and Lister. But while all that was taking place in one part of my mind, there was another part of me that was outside the box, somewhere else in the bitterly cold, dark, damp warehouse, looking down on a plastic bin and listening to the person inside talking to herself in different voices and occasionally laughing out loud as she desperately tried to hang on to her sanity.

Bob arrived later the next day. I suppose as it was Sunday he thought he would enjoy a bit of a lie-in. By the time he arrived I had been in the box for over eighteen hours.

'Have you got your blindfold on?'

'Yes.'

'Right, I'll get you out in a minute but before I do, the ten o'clock news will be coming on the radio. I want you to listen to the main stories and remember that they are for a tape we are going to make to send to your Mum and Dad.'

I was desperate for the loo by this time but felt I could hang on a few more minutes if it meant getting a message to Mum and Dad. God knows what they must be thinking by now. A couple of days earlier Bob had announced that he had been speaking to Kevin Watts who had confirmed that everything with regard to the ransom was going as planned. He had asked my parents' Christian names, which I told him were Warren and Betty. Initially, I was delighted, thinking that he must have been in touch with Shipways and that at least Mum and Dad would know something had happened; even the news that I had been kidnapped was better than no news at all, I reckoned. But later I wondered how seriously I could take Bob's claim to have spoken to Kevin and the question about my Mum and Dad could easily be part of the hoax.

The main news items on that Sunday morning concerned the release on bail of Imelda Marcos, and a new inquiry into the Zeebrugge ferry disaster of some months earlier. I told Bob all this as I ate my porridge but he seemed unimpressed as I hadn't really remembered enough details. There was quite a lot of coming and going in the other part of the warehouse which is probably why he put me back in the box. It was after one o'clock when he took me out again and we made the tape which he said he would play to Mum and Dad that very day.

The day before Bob had asked me which football team my father supported and I had told him our local team West Bromwich Albion. He decided that mention of how the team had got on in their league game the previous day would convince them the tape was a new one, proving I was still alive.

I sat on the hard-backed chair and he held the microphone towards my mouth as I repeated the words he told me to say:

'Hello, it's Stephanie here. They have allowed me to send a message to you, just to let you know that I am all right and unharmed. I hear that West Bromwich Albion lost yesterday to Swansea 3-2. I want you to know that I love you. I'm not to say too much but whatever the outcome, I'll always love you.'

Bob said I could add my own short message on to the end of the tape but reciting the words 'whatever the outcome, I'll always love you' had completely thrown me. They sounded so ominous that I couldn't concentrate on anything else, so I just tagged 'Look after the cats for me', on to the end of the words he had told me to repeat.

'Is that all you want to say?' he asked me, obviously surprised.

I nodded and muttered 'Yes.' I was completely choked.

He seemed to realise what had caused my distress because he immediately launched into an explanation. 'I know the message might sound a bit daunting but it is intended to keep them on their toes. You aren't going to be killed or even hurt, I've told you that haven't I?'

I nodded.

'Here.' He seemed exasperated by my reaction. 'Here,

feel this!' He took hold of my right hand and tapped it up and down on something soft.

'Do you know what these are?' he asked as he ran my hand over what felt like a box of something.

'No,' I said truthfully. I had no idea.

'They are your clothes,' he announced triumphantly. 'The clothes you came here in, all washed and ironed ready for you to go home. See, I told you didn't I? You are going home. Just as soon as this is over I'm going to drop you off near a police station and they will take you home. Do you believe me now?'

I nodded, for that moment I did believe him, but a box of clean clothes was not sufficient to hold the doubt and anguish at bay for very long. After I had made the tape Bob put me back in the box saying he was going to play the tape to Mum and Dad. He asked me if I wanted anything. Yes, I want something, I want to go home, you shit. I don't want to lie here locked up thinking about it while you just get into your car, drive to a telephone box and ring my house, the house where I live. But of course I didn't say any of that. I asked him to bring me a couple of bottles of pop to drink during the night because wherever he went and whatever he did, I knew exactly what was in store for me.

He was gone for a few hours, during which time I could think of nothing except what might be happening at home, which made me very tearful. I was terrified that I was close to losing my hold on the situation. I pictured the white telephone on the table in the hallway, remembered standing on the red fitted carpet just behind the front door and holding that same telephone for what must have amounted to hundreds of hours over the years. I wondered who would answer the call. It would be my Dad, I felt sure. What would Bob say? I hoped he wouldn't try to frighten them. Would my Dad know it was a tape recording? Of course he would. I knew it would be terrible for them to hear the message but comforted myself with the fact that at least they would know I was alive and Dad would reassure Mum with that thought, I felt sure.

'Well, what did they say?' I sat on the hard-backed chair while he prepared a mug of tomato soup for me.

'They didn't say anything, I didn't give them a chance. When a bloke answered the phone I made sure it were your Dad and then I played him the tape. Once it had finished I put the phone down.'

I wanted to be chatty and entertaining but simply couldn't summon up the necessary reserves.

'Come on, eat up,' he urged me, but I had no appetite for the soup and the by now stale bread left from the loaf he had bought for my arrival.

'I'm not very hungry today,' I told him, forcing a smile.

'You don't eat much, do you?'

'I'm just not hungry today, sorry.' You try a diet of porridge, tinned soup and stale bread and see how much of it you can shift after five days, I thought to myself, but I said nothing.

'I'll have to boil you up a big pot of stew with plenty of garlic in it,' he told me.

'I like garlic,' I told him. 'Do you?'

'Nah.' I knew he had shaken his head from the way the word came out. 'I don't like anything like that.'

When he asked me if I wanted to use the toilet, I knew he was preparing to put me into the box for the night. Although I had spent most of the day in there I didn't mind quite so much as I might have the day before. Making the tape and knowing that he had played it to my Dad somehow brought the whole crazy business into much sharper focus. Before today, what had gone on in the workshop had seemed almost like events taking place on a different planet. I didn't know where I was, which in a strange way prevented me from running a direct emotional line between this place and my real life. I could think about my Mum and Dad and my friends and my cats and feel sad but until that point it had been in an almost unreal way. Sitting on the chair and making the tape, knowing Bob had left the workshop, dialled my home on the telephone number I had given him and then come back to tell me about playing the tape to my Dad, made me realise that real life was still going on outside. Whatever I might have thought, I wasn't in some sort of time capsule, and today Bob had shuttled between the captivity that had become my world and the life which I had occupied until last Wednesday.

·7·

RADIO TWO, bursting into my consciousness at 8 am, heralded the end of what had been the worst weekend of my life so far. Never again would I complain about the lack of things to do at the weekend or the rubbish they put on the television on Saturday nights. The cold, the fear and the discomfort were intolerable but the boredom and the constant waiting were even more difficult to endure. Endless hours of waiting – for the sound of a car or a train passing, for the radio to come on or go off and, of course, for Bob, the biggest event of my day. His arrival brought with it food, drink, a chance to stretch my cramped limbs after hours crushed up in the box and most important of all, company.

In spite of all he had done I looked forward to his daily arrival as a child looks forward to Christmas morning.

I never lost sight of the fact that he was my captor and the person who continued to hold me against my will. I knew Bob was the obstacle standing between me and freedom. He was with me in the workshop for hours a day and could easily have put me back in his car and driven me to where he had picked me up from. Clearly he didn't want to do that, it was not part of the plan. But for all that he was also my lifeline, the person who released me from the box every day, provided me with food and drink, hot water to wash in, toilet facilities, bedding and clothes. Where would I have been without him? If one day he decided not to bother coming in I would be forced to stay in the box with nothing and no one. The long hours alone over the weekend had been a taste of what that would be like.

On the Monday morning I wanted to be cheerful and chatty when he arrived but the taped message I had made for my parents the previous day still weighed heavily on my mind. Despite Bob's reassurances I was not convinced everything would be all right, as he had promised, and despondency had set in hours before he took me out of the box at about 8.10 am. After giving me my usual break-fast and a bowl of hot water in which to wash my hands and face he provided me with a change of Y-fronts and a different pair of trousers.

He talked about the weather, telling me it was very foggy outside with poor visibility. This led on to a conver-sation about cars and I told him how I had always fancied a sports car but, for the moment, was very happy with the company car supplied by Shipways, a royal blue Ford Escort. I don't know whether or not he detected that I was feeling down but he suddenly asked me if I recalled the case of Suzy Lamplugh. I told him I remembered it well.

'That had nothing to do with me, you know,' he said with conviction.

Surprisingly, it hadn't occurred to me until then that the two cases might be linked. Once again Bob had man-aged to incite fear in a specific area where previously it had not existed. Now, I couldn't help but examine the similarities as he shuffled about the workshop.

'I'm going to have to go out in a while to phone Kevin

Watts,' he announced as I sat in silence on the hard-backed chair.

My heart leapt, as it did every time he mentioned anybody or anything linked with my normal life.

'All right,' I said calmly, although I felt anything but calm. This must be something to do with the ransom. Kevin had had a few days now to sort things out. My Mum and Dad had heard the tape the day before, which hopefully would convince them I was still alive, and they would all have been talking together. I still couldn't work out where the money to pay the ransom would come from. Bob seemed to think the fact that Shipways was owned by a large insurance company was enough to guarantee it. I was less convinced, but it was impossible for me to be sure about anything, so many unbelievable things had taken place over the last few days.

'It's very foggy outside so I'm not going to drive, but I shouldn't be too long, and all being well this will be your last night in the box. If everything goes to plan you will be going home on Wednesday. You can sleep on the mattress on Tuesday night. All right?'

Overcome by the prospect of getting out of the place I could only nod my head. Bob assumed a jokey tone as he said: 'I've enjoyed looking after you this week. It's been like taking care of a child. Are you sure you don't want to stay on a bit, have another week here?'

I shook my head and forced a smile. 'Thanks but no, that's an offer I will have to decline.'

He laughed to himself as he moved about the building. At the time I was happy to have brought a smile to his face, but recalling the incident now I am filled with rage that he could make a joke about something so vital to me. I was never convinced anything he told me was true. I tried hard to believe him when he said I would be freed, because for those few scant moments I could enjoy some piece of mind, but always lurking in the background was the fear that I was never going to be released. For all I knew he had been holding Suzy Lamplugh captive in his workshop before he kidnapped me. And what did he mean, he had enjoyed looking after me this week? I continually consoled myself with the fact that taking care of me must be causing considerable disruption to his daily life. But maybe he didn't have much of a life to disrupt, perhaps having somebody locked up in a box was a distraction for him, something to help pass the time while he was at work. I didn't know what to think or believe.

During the time he was away I lay in the box mapping out the workshop in my mind. If I ever get out of here, I thought, I want to be able to provide the police with a full description of the place in which I'm being held. I felt that the box was in a corner at the end of the workshop, as far away as I could be from what I imagined was the shop area, where I frequently heard the sound of conversation and the ring of an old-fashioned till. I knew a metal door on metal runners was the main entrance to the place and that the walls of the building were of stone, rough and unfinished, with no attempt made to smooth them over with plaster, and I knew the floor was concrete. That morning, before Bob had arrived, I had pushed my head up against the lid of the bin and peeped through the very narrow crack that opened up. I could see the ceiling above the box. It seemed quite high and there was a wooden beam running widthways across it.

Bob had told me there was no running water in the building but I knew there must be electricity because of the tools he used, the lights, the kettle and the microwave that heated my meals. What sounded like an old-style telephone was somewhere to my left but during the time I had been there it had rung only twice and when Bob

153 Turnberry Road, where Stephanie was kidnapped by Michael Sams. *(Mirror Syndication International – MSI)*

A replica of the Cloth of Veronica, which Stephanie first saw in Godshill Church on the Isle of Wight. This image came to Stephanie during her first night as a captive in the box.

Stephanie worked closely with the police to produce this artist's impression of her abductor, which was carried by most national newspapers just three days after her release from the workshop. *(News Team International)*

Stephanie's first impression of Michael Sams was of an ordinary, fairly grubby, little man. *(MSI)*

Above: A re-creation of the area in which Stephanie was held and, below, the actual interior of Sams' workshop. *(MSI; Hulton/Reuters)*

Stephanie at the press conference in Birmingham only hours after her release. *(Press Association)*

With her pet cockatiel and her best friend and flat-mate Stacey Kettner, who has been 'a constant source of humour and support' to Stephanie since the trial.

Stephanie outside her family home in Great Barr, with parents Betty and Warren. *(MSI)*

Leeds teenager Julie Dart was kidnapped and murdered by Michael Sams six months before Stephanie was abducted. *(Hulton/Reuters)*

Stephanie with her cat Swiftnick before leaving Birmingham to begin a new life on the Isle of Wight. *(Peter Corns/Daily Express)*

answered it, the conversations had lasted no more than a few seconds.

Bob wasn't very communicative on his return in the afternoon. He said that everything seemed to be going to plan and that he would be speaking to Kevin again the next day. He told me that he had work to catch up with as he had lost time 'running about' that morning. I spent the rest of the afternoon in the box, waiting and wondering if he would be more forthcoming when he took me out of the box for my evening meal. By this stage I was spending almost all the time locked up as Bob went about his business.

Later, I sat on the hard-backed chair wanting to ask a hundred questions but fearing to begin. I had selected tomato soup, a personal favourite, from the menu that evening.

'Do you want bread or toast?'

'Bread, please.'

'Some of these feel a bit stale,' he said. I imagined he was sorting through some of the outer slices of the loaf. 'The ones in the middle seem better.'

Following the ping of the microwave Bob presented me with a mug of soup and a couple of slices of white bread without butter. His earlier promise of organising some proper food hadn't materialised: it had been porridge every morning and soup every evening so far. He supplemented this diet with two-fingered Kit Kat bars, giving me three or four at a time. I had never eaten so much chocolate.

Finally, just when I had almost come to terms with the idea that he wasn't going to mention anything about his conversation with Kevin, he announced that this would indeed be my last night in the box.

'Really?'

'Yes, looks like it. I will have to speak to Kevin Watts again tomorrow, just to check he's got the money, but it seems like we're in business. You'll be back with your

Mum and Dad in a couple of days if all goes according to plan.'

I was aware of him speaking about the plan and something about what his mate had said, but even talk of the dreaded mate didn't have the power to shake my extraordinary feelings of elation. So, it was really going to happen! Bob had spoken to Kevin and Kevin had said things were going according to plan; I was going to be set free. The money would be paid and Bob would let me go, somewhere near a hospital or a police station. I imagined walking down a road somewhere and coming towards me there would be a single policeman, a regular bobby with a dark blue hat. I would stop him and tell him that I had just been released after being kidnapped. He would take me home to my Mum and Dad and soon all this would be forgotten and my life would be back to normal. I knew I would have to talk to the police about what had happened but after that my life would be my own again. Back to normal!

It was almost as if he had read my thoughts.

'When you are released the police will want to know everything you remember.'

Oh no, don't let him get cold feet about releasing me in case I give the game away.

'Will they?'

'Yes, they'll question you about everything.'

'I won't say anything,' I tried to reassure him.

'There's no point thinking that. They will get it out of you, anything, everything you know. They're clever like that. You might as well tell them the truth.'

'Well, there isn't really much I can tell them.' Surely, he must realise that. I hadn't seen him since the morning at Turnberry Road, I didn't know where I was – I wasn't, I reckoned, what anyone would consider star witness material.

'Will you tell them about, you know, that?' he continued. I instinctively knew he meant the rape.

I shook my head.

'Not that it were much anyway.'

Not that it were much? I could hardly believe my ears. Surely, I had misheard him. How is it possible to rape someone and then decide that the act didn't amount to much? I wondered how he thought it was possible to measure the damage. What would a rape that 'were something' involve, in his book?

I was annoyed to find that silent tears were pouring down my face. I couldn't believe that all the fear and horror of that first night, the overwhelming feelings of humiliation and degradation I had struggled to keep at bay during those endless hours in the box, could be dismissed so easily. But I was also aware that Bob's words had echoed what I had constantly tried to convince myself of. Just put it out of your mind, I had repeatedly told myself; it's all over now, and it could have been worse. Suddenly I knew for certain that it couldn't have been worse. It could have been different: he could have beaten me up first, he could have hurt me more during the rape itself. That would have made it different, but it wouldn't have made it worse. I'd lain on the mattress in a state of utter terror – stripped naked, with my hands and arms immobilised by handcuffs and held above my head, the blindfold adding a further dimension to my fear. If I had been attacked on a quiet road at night the outcome may well have been the same but at least I would have had an opportunity to try to defend myself. If I had been in a situation where I could have lashed out with my arms and legs, screamed and scratched, then I would at least have the satisfaction of knowing I had retaliated. But as it was, the awful thought that I had lain there and let it happen wouldn't go away. I couldn't think of any way I could have stopped it happening but could I have put up more of a struggle? The terror of being killed was, at that time, uppermost in my mind. I didn't want to make him angry again. I had seen where that led in the bathroom at Turnberry Road. But I was damned if I was going to accept his account of events. He might have my body captive but my mind was free and it was clear. I had been attacked and I had also been raped and whatever I might say to him about it I was not prepared to diminish what had happened in my own mind.

'I won't say anything about it to anyone,' I told him, still in tears.

'I would deny it anyway,' he snapped, and I heard him walk away to another part of the workshop.

Later, as he took the empty soup mug from me, his tone was softer.

'They will probably offer you psychiatric help after all this is finished. You take it, take whatever they offer. Go back to your job and get on with your life. Don't let this ruin things for you. You've done nothing. You're just an innocent victim and you're going to go home. After this is done with, after you, I'm going to give this up. It's not worth it.'

I could tell he was standing directly in front of me. As I stood up the chain around my ankle rattled. He was saying all the right things, that I was an innocent victim, that I was going home and should get on with my life. But could I believe him? I was desperate for reassurance and some form of human contact, even from him, the person responsible for it all.

'Can I give you a hug?' I asked.

'What?' He sounded incredulous.

'Can I give you a hug?' I held out my arms towards him. 'It will be all right won't it? I am going home, aren't I, please say I am?'

I pulled him into my arms. 'Aye, it will be all right,' he said. For just a split second my cheek touched his as we embraced and I noticed he wasn't wearing glasses. I must remember that, I thought.

In the box that night I had the strangest dream. I seemed to drift in and out of sleep all night. At one point I saw, in a dream, a medieval village. As I approached it I saw there were a number of low, thatched buildings, near which children were dancing around a maypole. Watching them from his position on the wall of the well and occasionally shouting encouragement was an elderly man dressed in a jester's costume. He looked very impressive in his coloured costume with bells and holding a pig's bladder. As I got closer I realised that the man was Frankie Howerd, the comedian. He pulled his face in a series of typically Frankie Howerd expressions, thrusting out his lips and raising his eyebrows, but I didn't laugh. Instead I asked him very seriously: 'Am I going to live? Am I going to be all right through all this? What am I going to do? Am I going to die?'

'Oh no, no, you're not going to die,' he said in that 'no, no missus' voice he always used. He spread his hands out in front of him and some of the bells on his jester's costume tinkled slightly.

'No, no, you're going to be just fine.' He shook with laughter as he added: 'I'm going to go this year. I'm going to die this year but don't you worry about me my dear, you'll be all right and that's all that matters.'

I asked him a number of times if he was quite sure and he laughed and chatted and was insistent that everything would turn out all right in the end.

When I awoke I was immensely comforted. I felt as if I had had a real conversation with someone. I knew it was a dream but it felt so real that it truly seemed as if I had been speaking to Frankie Howerd and that he had reassured me that I wasn't going to die. Not in a serious way but in a friendly, kindly, jokey way that almost made me feel a bit silly for having thought such a thing in the first place. I had always liked the man and enjoyed his humour and although I cannot think what put the picture of him in that ridiculous jester's outfit in my mind, 'talking' with him that night was a real boost to my morale and it did, crazy as it sounds, give me a sort of courage to face the coming days.

I was awake long before the radio came on at eight o'clock next morning. Before he had left the night before Bob had said it would be my last night in the box and that I would be going home on Wednesday. I still couldn't be certain he was telling the truth but I badly wanted to believe him. I finished off the last of the two cans of pop he had left me. Since I had told him how thirsty I got in the box during the night he made sure I had a couple of cans and a couple of bars of chocolate each evening before leaving. I liked to think of this as a sign he was protecting his investment, keeping me fed and healthy for the time when he would exchange me for the ransom money. On a good day, it almost convinced me that I would be going home.

I lay contemplating the prospect as the radio came on. Not long after that Bob arrived. As always I was stiff as I slid out of the coffin in the morning. He held my hands as I ran up and down on the spot for two or three minutes. His hands were square and his small, fat fingers were hairy on the back. I tried to involve Bob in a chat about what had happened in *Coronation Street* the previous night, but he was uncommunicative. Before half-past eight, after my usual breakfast of porridge and tea, a visit to the loo and a quick wash, I was back in the box. It was always disappointing when, after I had spent hours alone, Bob wasn't in the mood to talk. Sometimes what he said upset me, particularly talk about his mate, which cropped up at least once or twice a day, yet even that was preferable to no conversation at all.

I'm sure the very thought of holding a conversation with a man who had attacked, kidnapped and raped you will seem completely crazy to some people. I can only say that unless you are in that situation you cannot imagine how it feels. I had decided from the outset that I would try to establish a rapport with him, try to get him to see me as a human being. Also, I was totally dependent on him for food, drink and the carrying out of every other bodily function. I didn't want to offend him. But it became something more than that. His was the only real voice I heard during that long and lonely period of time. Of course there was talking on the radio and there were muffled conversations when people came into the other part of the workshop, but it was Bob and Bob alone who provided me with a human link to the outside world.

During the night hours as I lay locked in the cold dark coffin, I knew that all the time I was locked up there he was out in the real world. He was driving his car through streets where the shop windows would be filled with lights and notices announcing the January sales, past pubs and wine bars, past television rental shops with five or six sets playing to empty streets. He would go home to the big, white house with the greenhouse he had told me about, fill a kettle, open the fridge, switch on the telly. When he left me I knew he was doing all the ordinary things most of us do when we get home in the evening. Talking with him brought those things closer to me. Hearing about what went on outside my four walls made me feel more a part of real life even if it was by proxy.

At one point in the afternoon he turned down the radio

and told me, through the lid of the bin, that he was going out to make a phone call. Twenty or so minutes later, just after the three o'clock news, I heard the metal door being pulled closed but as I didn't hear his car I imagined he must be walking to his destination. He returned after about two hours and took me out of the box for my evening meal.

After his walk Bob seemed much more relaxed than he had been earlier in the day. 'Are you sure you want to go?' he asked me again. 'I've enjoyed having you here.'

'Sorry, 'fraid I must,' I replied.

'I've just been talking to Kevin Watts at Shipways. Who is David by the way?'

'David?'

'Yes. When I was speaking to Kevin Watts at first I could hear a voice in the background and then he yelled "Dave, get out!"'

'Oh, that must have been David the financial adviser. He works with us in the office.'

'It sounded a bit funny, that's all,' he sounded thankful. 'I wouldn't be surprised if Kevin Watts had been in touch with the police.'

'I don't think he would,' I stammered. I couldn't bear anything to go wrong at this stage. 'Not if you told him not to.'

But Bob didn't seem to have heard me. 'Mind you, I've suspected all along that they were involved,' he muttered.

As I sipped from the mug of very hot vegetable soup I was aware of a lot of activity going on around me.

'I'm just getting your bedding ready for tonight,' he told me. 'Remember I said you would be sleeping on the mattress? I'm just sorting out your pillows and blankets.'

I was delighted. Even though the adjustments Bob had made to the wooden coffin-shaped box inside the wheely bin had been a huge improvement after the first night, my movements were still very restricted. I could only lie on my back. It was impossible to roll over on to my side or my stomach. As I considered the joys of being free to move about I heard Bob dragging something across the floor. It sounded suspiciously like another mattress. I followed its progress across the workshop with my head. By this time I had realised that though I couldn't see, my nose and ears were more finely tuned than they had been before I had been forced to rely on them so heavily. I couldn't smell anything but it definitely sounded like another mattress being dragged along behind him. Bob must have noticed my interest.

'It's for me,' he explained. 'I'm going to stay here with you tonight. You're not going to be tied, I'm going to trust you, but I warn you, don't betray my trust. I'll be lying here beside you all night so don't try anything.'

Perhaps I should have been frightened at the prospect of Bob staying overnight on a mattress only six inches from the one I was sleeping on. But it was the thought of not having to go into the box, of sleeping on the mattress completely unrestricted, that filled my conscious mind. I was childishly delighted at the thought.

·8·

I LAY ON the mattress listening to Bob moving about the workshop. He had given me a quilt, a blanket and two pillows and although I still had my blindfold on, he had removed all the other bonds. I had to resist the temptation to squirm about with joy. No handcuffs, no chains and, best of all, no box. I heard him put something down between the mattresses.

'There's some pop for you,' he said. 'There's Lucozade and lemonade.'

'Thanks.'

I heard him lowering himself on to the mattress just a few inches away from me.

'It's really foggy out there tonight. I don't know how we will go on for collecting the money tomorrow if this keeps up. You can hardly see your hand in front of your face,' he complained.

Until that moment it hadn't occurred to me that something as fickle as the weather might play a part in whether or not I was to be allowed to go home. I felt I had explored every other scenario in my mind's eye over the last few days. But fog – who ever considers fog? Yet I knew that more than cold or any amount of rain, fog could prevent things running smoothly. If Bob and his mate had arranged to pick the money up fairly locally it would mean that Kevin, who Bob had said would be 'dropping' the ransom, might be delayed, ruining everything. Alternatively, if Bob and his mate were collecting the money from the Birmingham area, they would have miles to travel on fog-bound roads. The thought that everything might have to be postponed for another day or even longer horrified me.

'Perhaps it will have cleared by the morning,' I said, trying to reassure myself as much as him.

'Aye, I suppose it might, we'll just have to see.'

We continued to chat about the weather, a little more about astronomy, and about television programmes. I felt he enjoyed talking and being listened to. There was, I felt, something lonely about him: perhaps it was just working on his own all day that made him glad of my company. Whatever his reasons I believed him when he said that he would miss having me around. But since I didn't want him to get any ideas about hanging on to me I turned the conversation round to how much I was looking forward to getting home to see Mum and Dad and my cats.

However, Bob had obviously been thinking about our conversation of the day before, when I had assured him I would not talk to the police, and now he took up the topic again. Most of what I had said was a lie: ever since he had taken me prisoner I had been trying to catalogue each and every detail of what went on in order to tell the police.

'When all this gets out you'll be a celebrity, you know,' he suddenly announced.

'What do you mean?' I asked.

'When this story gets out, in the papers and that, I'll bet you will have them all around asking for your story . . . the press, newspapers and television. You'll have the police as well, of course, but the papers will definitely be round once this gets out.'

'I won't say anything,' I repeated determinedly. 'I won't tell them a thing.'

'Course you will,' he replied quietly.

Oh my God, oh my God, I thought again, don't let him think that. Please don't let him think I'm going to blab to the police because if he does I've had it, he will kill me for sure.

'I won't tell, really, I won't.'

'It will be easier for you in the long run if you do. Tell them what you know and then you tell your story to the papers or write a book about what's happened. You should make a load of money and become a star.'

I was well aware that although Bob had displayed moments of concern, even tenderness, as he did when he bathed my cold, sore feet, he was still a bad and dangerous man and not one who should be allowed to roam the streets. If I should get out of this alive I would do everything in my power to prevent it happening to some other innocent woman. If Bob could do this once and get away with it the chances were he would try it again. And even if, as he had said, he was going to 'finish with all this' after me, by which I assumed he meant his life of crime, there was always his mate, and there was no way in the world I felt that man should be given the benefit of the doubt. Yes, if I made it the police would have all the help I could give them. I wanted both Bob and his mate caught and punished for what they had done to me. I wanted them off the streets for a long, long time.

There was silence as these thoughts went through my head. No doubt Bob thought I was seeing myself in my new role as celebrity kidnap victim. Perhaps he thought it would compensate for what had happened. Although even as the thought went through my mind I knew beyond a shadow of a doubt that I couldn't and wouldn't tell the police about the rape.

I couldn't bear the thought of anyone knowing. If I told the police they would want to know all the details: every sordid humiliating moment would have to be recounted, perhaps more than once. And if Bob was caught and charged he would probably, as he had said, 'deny it anyway', which would would mean the whole lot coming out. I would have to tell the judge, lawyers, the jury – all of them would have to know. And I would have to say it all in open court, in front of him but worse, far worse than that, in front of my Mum and Dad.

Nor could I begin to think what any of this would do to Mum. I knew my Dad would be frantic but somehow he would cope, he's that type of man. But Mum was different: there was no way I could let her hear anything more awful than the things she would have to hear anyway.

The thought suddenly occurred to me that they might not believe it was rape. It would be Bob's word against mine. When it happened I had been terrified that he was going to kill me. He had already attacked and cut me at Turnberry Road, and I didn't know what else he was capable of. But if he said that I hadn't put up a fight, that I had done everything he told me to do, that I had not fought or kicked or screamed, that I had just let him do what he wanted, then he would be right. I had lain there, had not tried to stop him. I would have done anything to prevent him becoming angry again but would the judge and the jury believe that? How could they possibly know how scared I had been, how terrified that each hour would be my last? I had read countless newspaper stories of alleged rape victims who had not been believed. Smart defence lawyers tying them up in knots on the witness stand, making it seem as if the victim was somehow responsible for the attack, as if she had invited it. I knew that by using their skills they could make perfectly ordinary women look like sluts.

No, I would tell the police everything I could to help them find Bob but they didn't need to know about the rape. I didn't want anyone thinking that the grubby, insignificant little man I remembered from Turnberry Road had been anywhere near me. Nobody needed to know about that, and they wouldn't, not if I had anything to do with it.

I was so deep in thought that I almost jumped when Bob spoke.

'I'm going to turn the light out. When I do you can take your blindfold off but remember I will be lying here, right next to you, all night, so don't try anything. I'm going to trust you but I'm warning you, don't betray that trust.'

I had heard all this before but I shook my head sagely: 'I won't.'

Honestly, what an idiot! Did he seriously think that after all I had been through I would take a chance on blowing everything now, the night before I was due to be released?

'Right, you can open your eyes now but remember what I said.'

'I will.'

'And in the morning when the radio comes on I don't want you to open your eyes. As soon as you hear the radio put your blindfold back on straightaway, do you understand?'

'Yes.'

I pulled the blindfold off and held it in my hand. I squinted in the darkness. High about my head a small red light flickered. No sooner had I focused on it than Bob groaned. 'Oh, I forgot about that!'

'What?' I asked.

'That red light up there, you weren't supposed to see that.'

111

'What light?' I asked trying to sound drowsy. 'I haven't opened my eyes yet. I'm very tired. Anyway, it doesn't matter, does it?' I mumbled the words and for the first night in ages, enjoyed the luxury of rolling over on to my side.

It was freezing during the night, and I realised that being in the bin must have protected me from a lot of the cold. The heat of my body and breath in such a confined space probably helped increase the temperature quite a bit above that in the rest of the workshop. Although I was fully clothed and completely wrapped in the quilt Bob had given me, I still felt cold and my face was icy. The only way I could bear it was to sleep with the blanket pulled right up over my face.

At one point I sat up to have a drink from the can of Lucozade Bob had given me. Although he did not speak, I was aware that he was wide awake. I could feel him shift position as I sat up; perhaps he thought I was about to make a bid for freedom and was getting ready to bring me down with a rugby tackle. Although he didn't speak I was aware of a tension in the space between us until he heard the burst of escaping air as I opened the ring-pull can and put it to my lips. I didn't feel as if I slept at all that night, although I probably dozed. I was constantly aware of Bob's proximity and felt that he too was awake. I didn't attempt to brave the cold and have another sip of the can of Lucozade. Eventually, I pulled the quilt up over my head and settled down to wait for morning.

As instructed by Bob I pulled the blindfold back over my eyes as soon as I heard the radio come on. I was charged with a feeling of enormous excitement. This was the day I was to be released. I would never spend another night in this wretched place; in a few hours I would be home and in a few days all this would seem like a bad dream.

'You were very restless last night,' Bob said.

'Was I? I hope I didn't disturb you,' I answered. It was true. I hoped he would be fit to get me back home. I didn't want him too tired to drive me to Birmingham.

As he prepared breakfast he chatted animatedly. I rose from the mattress, made my way to the makeshift lavatory with his help, and then sat on the hard-backed chair.

'Huh, this seems to be the last of the porridge.'

'Well, you have it,' I offered, again with the thought in mind that he needed all his strength to get through the day and get me home.

'No, you have it,' he insisted. 'If you don't finish it all I'll have what you leave.'

I had a few spoonfuls and left the rest which he appeared to eat. As I swallowed the hot, strong tea he gave me, he explained that today being 'the big day' he would have a lot to do. He told me that I would be in the box all day because he had several phone calls to make and other things to attend to. I didn't relish the prospect of hours and hours in the box but I knew they would have to be endured if I was to get out of there that night.

'I was thinking that it would be nice to have a photograph of you,' Bob suddenly said. 'You know, something to remember you by.'

Weird, I thought, definitely weird, but my voice gave no indication of what was going on in my head.

'Yes, all right, if you want. Have you got a camera here?' I enquired chirpily.

'Yes, I brought one in with me yesterday. Sit over on the mattress and take your blindfold off, but don't open your eyes.'

I passed him my empty cup and did as he asked, making my way slowly over to the mattress, where I sat down. I took my blindfold off and attempted a watery smile. This was beyond belief. I began having serious thoughts about

113

Bob's sanity. I hadn't noticed any obvious signs of madness but then this whole thing was mad, wasn't it? Only somebody completely crazy would embark upon something like this. And now he wanted a photograph.

The temptation to open my eyes was huge but I kept them shut. I was aware of a flash and within seconds he was helping me replace the blindfold.

'Are you all right?' he asked as I got up from the mattress a little shakily.

'My foot hurts,' I complained.

After removing my boot and sock Bob told me that one of my toes had become red and sore looking. He told me to take off the other boot and he would wash my feet for me. As he was doing this, he took my socks, which were damp, and put them over the heater. He waited until they were completely dry before putting them back on, then he told me I would have to go back into the box.

He handed me the seed tray toilet. 'I will have to pop back in a few hours but I won't have time to mess about taking you to the toilet. After that I won't be back until tonight, probably not until eight or nine o'clock, so take it just in case.'

He then gave me five two-fingered Kit Kat bars and a can of lemonade.

I tried to think positively. I wanted the day to go smoothly and I knew that there was no way he would let me remain on the mattress for all the hours it would take to organise things. Yet the thought of being squashed back into that awful wooden coffin filled me with dread. I realised Bob had probably let me sleep on the mattress the night before because I would be spending such a long time in the box; but having had the freedom to move my limbs freely all night made the thought of so many hours of physical restriction even worse. There was nothing else for it I thought as I eased my way in. This time tomorrow it will all be over. I prayed that day as I have never prayed in my life before or since.

Bob went out at about 9.15 am saying that he would be back around midday, which he was. Just before he left a second time, he turned the radio down and spoke through the locked lid of the bin:

'Right, I'm off now. My mate's here and we are going to pick up the money. I won't be back until tonight. I've got to be here by nine o'clock for a phone call, just to confirm that everything is all right. Then I'll get you back home, okay?'

'Yes, all right. Has the fog gone this morning?' I asked hopefully.

'No, it's still really bad but I reckon we'll manage.'

'Well, drive carefully,' I said. I could hear the anxiety in my own voice. The thought that the fog might somehow prevent things going ahead as planned still scared the life out of me. Perhaps responding to that anxiety and wanting to put my mind at rest Bob announced:

'Don't worry, I've got a note in my wallet. If anything happens to me, if there is a traffic accident or something else that means I won't be coming back, then the note will be found explaining all about you and you will be rescued. Do you understand?'

'Yes.'

'Right then, I'm off. See you later.'

'Yes, bye then.'

I lay in the darkness. I had pulled my blindfold off as soon as Bob had locked the bin lid but he must have turned the workshop lights out because only the faintest trace of light filtered through the round ventilation holes in the side of the bin. I didn't know whether to believe his story of carrying a note about me or not. I hoped it was true, but maybe he had said that to prevent me lying there for hours worrying that he might be killed in the fog and I would never be found. It was always impossible to know what was really going on in his mind. I constantly struggled with the hope that he was telling the truth, balanced against the probability that he wasn't.

For the next seven or eight hours my thoughts were almost constantly with Bob. In my own interests I had to hope that his mad scheme was going to succeed; in an odd sort of way I was on his side. If everything went according to plan he would collect the money and take me home. If it didn't – well, I didn't want to think about that. I wondered if Kevin had managed to get through the fog? What would happen if Shipways had brought in the police and Bob was caught: would he tell them where I was, or would he and his mate say nothing until it was too late? I tried to concentrate on other things but nothing worked.

Only the news, broadcast every hour by Radio Two, permeated my thoughts. Each time I heard a news bulletin I was aware that another hour had passed, another hour closer to nine o'clock, Bob's return and freedom. It seemed I recorded the passing of every hour over a period of a hundred years.

I had long since finished the can of lemonade and all but one of the chocolate bars. I wasn't hungry but eating and drinking were a way of passing the time: pacing myself with a finger of Kit Kat was another way of celebrating the passage of time. Bob had said he had to be back by nine o'clock for a phone call. I had decided to eat the last Kit Kat at 8.30, then if I ate slowly and he arrived a bit early, I would not be lying there worrying for the last half hour.

By quarter-past nine I had finished the chocolate but there was no sign of Bob; neither had there been a telephone call, as he had expected, at nine o'clock. I had been suppressing feelings of impotence, fear and rage, to the best of my ability, all day. These emotions had been with me throughout the time I had spent in the workshop but some sixth sense told me that any display of them would be entirely inappropriate when Bob was around. This day, however, had been different: I had been on a knife-edge since Bob had left the building some nine hours or so earlier.

At first I tried to speak calmly to myself. It was January: the roads might be icy. Fog had made visibility difficult, which would slow everybody and everything down. It wasn't surprising he was a bit late. I attempted to use this line of reasoning with myself until half-past nine but as the minutes passed I could feel my panic mounting. By the time the ten o'clock news was over I was completely frantic. I was convinced that something serious had happened to Bob.

'I'm never going to see him again. He's not coming back and I'm going to die in here.' I spoke the words out loud. Now everything was black, not a trace of light filtered through the air-holes; I lay in the darkness with my fear. I tried to push the lid of the bin open but it was obviously securely locked. Even so I began banging on it – lifting my arms up and behind, as I lay on my back, I thumped as hard as I could. It occurred to me that should Bob come back and hear me thumping he might easily kill me for trying to escape but the fear of being left in the bin to rot was even greater than my fear of Bob. I continued to thump and bang on the bin lid but to no effect. I could feel my body begin to shake as it had on my first night in captivity and, despite the below-freezing temperature outside, I started to perspire. I tried to sit up but got myself jammed and only by a huge effort managed to free myself. There was just no way out at all.

I lay back panting. He wasn't coming back, that was obvious. Either he had collected the ransom and, with no

117

further need of me, he and his mate had decided to take the money and run, or there had been some sort of accident, a road accident or maybe something involving the police, and he was lying dead or unconscious, unable to tell anyone where I was. Well, I'm not going to lie here and starve to death, I decided. There is no way I can lie here waiting to die, not after all these hours, all these awful, endless days. I would kill myself first. I pulled the quilt right up and over my face. I would suffocate myself.

I pressed the soft material of the duvet into my face and tried to hold my breath but it was completely futile. I couldn't kill myself, I didn't want to die. I was crying by now, huge sobs of despair and, in between offering up prayers, trying to plea bargain with God. 'Please, please get me out of here alive, please. I will go to church every Sunday and I'll pray every day. I'll be a better person in every way if you'll just get me out.' I was completely pathetic: all the control I had worked at maintaining since Turnberry Road was suddenly no longer there. All the fears I had worked at keeping right at the back of my mind had collectively pushed their way to the front.

As I lay sobbing and shaking I felt the switch Bob had given me early in my captivity. With all the thumping and rattling around I had been doing it had somehow worked its way under my shoulder. It was a sort of light switch, a rectangular box about as long as my little finger, like the ones sometimes found on torches. He had told me if I pressed it, a red light would be illuminated in the other part of the workshop, the part where I sometimes heard him speaking with people.

'When I see the light go on I will know you want me for summat and I'll come in to you.'

Remembering his words I pressed the switch on and off frantically. I knew there was nobody out there to see it and imagining a small red light flickering on and off in the darkness, the only sign that I was in there, merely compounded my fear. He wasn't coming back, he had got his money and done a runner, I was convinced of that now. God knows how long it will take them to find me, dead in this box, my only communication with the outside world a little red light shining somewhere in the vastness of a deserted workshop miles away from anywhere. I would do it this time. I didn't want to go through days and days of this. I wrapped myself up in the quilt and pressed the material against my mouth and nose. But much as I wanted to lose consciousness, I couldn't prevent myself pushing down the quilt and gasping for air.

As I sucked in a long lungful I thought I heard a car in the distance. I pushed the quilt down to my waist and shook my hair back from my head. Yes, it was. Oh God, oh God, oh God, please, please let it be him! I strained to hear the vehicle come closer, biting my knuckle to stop myself screaming out loud.

The car stopped. I heard one door slam shut and moments later the big old metal door was pulled open. A light came on in the workshop and my heart began to race. Whoever this was they had come for me. Bob, his mate, the police, whoever they were, they were not leaving the building without me.

·9·

I heard footsteps; the radio was turned down.

'Are you all right?'

It was Bob, the man who had brought me here and made me endure all this, the person wholly responsible for the unquantifiable pain and mental anguish I had suffered, and yet – how can I explain? – his voice that night was the sweetest sound I had ever heard.

I was an emotional wreck. 'Yes, I'm all right, please just get me out of here!'

'Just a minute, I'll only be a few minutes and then we'll have you out.'

'Have you got the money?'

'Yes.'

'Can I go home then? Please will you get me out?'

'Hold on.'

He banged and clattered about for what seemed like an eternity but was in fact probably no more than a few minutes. The lid was opened and I shot out in a single movement.

I was in a state of collapse, unable to stand up without his support. I was crying, shaking, blabbering in my distress.

'Have you got the money? Can I go home now? Please can I go now?'

'Sshh, it's all right. Yes you're going home now. Just calm down. We have to change our clothes and then we are leaving straight away. I'm putting your own clothes on the chair here. Take off everything you are wearing and leave them on the floor and put your own things back on.'

I felt the pile of my things and immediately started to take off all the clothes he had given me to wear. Next to me I could hear rustling and assumed that, as he had said, he was changing his clothes as well. I was too excited at the prospect of going home to wonder whether or not he was watching me this time.

When I was wearing my own things he asked me if I wanted to wash my face. I did so quickly but told him I wouldn't bother with my hair. The hairbrush he let me use was far from efficient on my shock of waist-length hair and I didn't want to waste a single second of time. I just wanted to be off. I stood quietly and waited until he came towards me and took my arm.

'Come on then, you're going home.'

He walked me slowly towards the door, advising me where to step up over the step. I felt I was in a sheltered spot, maybe a carport, because I couldn't feel the wind I had so often heard whistling around the building. But the night air was so cold that I could feel my lips and nose beginning to go numb in the few seconds it took for him to secure the door; at the same time it was wonderful, so sweet and clean it almost had a taste to it.

Bob helped me into the car. I was still blindfolded but apart from asking me to lean my head on a pillow arrangement he had fixed up around the seatbelt, presumably to obscure my face from view, and telling me to wrap a cardigan around my head he seemed quite happy to leave me as I was, without handcuffs or ropes.

It was cold in the car and I shivered violently.

'What's up?' he asked.

'I'm just a bit cold.'

'Here,' he said pulling something from the back seat of the car and putting it on my lap. 'It's your coat, put it over your legs. I've put your brooch in the pocket. Be careful when you pull your gloves out that you don't lose it.'

Apart from the pillow he had arranged to shield my face, I was sitting up in the car quite normally, unlike when he'd brought me to the workshop. This time the seat was upright and I was not restricted in any way. My blindfold would have been the only indication to an observer that there was anything amiss.

He started the car and we progressed slowly along the same dirt track I remembered travelling on the day I was kidnapped. I reached into my coat pocket: sure enough my leather gloves were tucked in there and, right at the bottom, the brooch I had been using to secure my scarf before Bob told me to take it off at Turnberry Road, because he wanted to use it first to tie my hands together and later as a blindfold.

A chill went through me as I remembered that morning. I turned my gloves over and over in the pocket of my coat until I found it. There it was, just below the index finger of the right glove: the tear where the knife had penetrated my hand. The wound was still stiff and a bit sore but I had stopped associating it with the fight at Turnberry Road. Feeling it now brought the whole episode back to me, and the images made me very uncomfortable.

Bob was oblivious to what was going on in my mind as he rattled on about the events of that evening.

'You wouldn't believe how many police there were around when I brought you here.'

What on earth did he expect me to say to that? 'Congratulations, Bob! You managed to outwit them all and keep me prisoner for all this time without being sussed out!' I just mumbled 'Oh, really', or something equally non-committal. I wasn't out of the woods yet and wouldn't be until I was sitting in the lounge at home. I must remember that.

'All right, you can take the cardigan off your head now.'

I could tell we were travelling quite fast along country roads and was slightly concerned that I wasn't wearing a seat belt. After all my earlier thoughts about traffic accidents I was possibly a bit paranoid.

'Do you think I need a seat belt on?' I asked tentatively. I didn't want to start fumbling about trying to put it on without his permission in case he thought I was trying to find the door handle to attempt a runner.

'No, you'll be all right, just stay down in the seat. There isn't a lot of traffic about.'

After travelling for about two miles I heard him click the heater on and the car became warmer immediately. We seemed to be travelling on a dual carriageway now; there were no obvious bends in the road and I guessed we were travelling at around seventy-five miles an hour. He didn't at any time seem to be panicking but he had definitely been making haste since arriving back at the workshop. I thought that perhaps he was still working to some sort of deadline, although his conversation was relaxed.

'Is the fog still bad?' I asked, hoping it had lifted and we were not hurtling into the unknown at this speed.

'Yes. My mate fell off his bike three times when we did the pick-up because of it. And British Rail have put up a fence that wasn't there when we did the practice pick-up run. That held us up a bit.'

'But you managed?'

'Yes, we managed. I checked the cash with a special

device to make sure it wasn't marked, and it isn't, so now you're going home just like I said.'

'It was all there then?'

'Yes – apart from the weather causing a few spills everything went according to plan. Mind you, I don't expect my mate will hang on to his share for long. It will all be spent in a few months, he's that sort of bloke.'

'And what about you?'

'No, I plan to save my share, I'm not what you might call a spendthrift.'

We travelled on for a while in silence as I considered my luck in not having met his horrible mate. I had been terrified that he would appear at some point. All the things Bob said about him, and the discovery of the kinky underwear in the bottom of the bin, made me know I was very fortunate to have escaped him.

'I'm going to stop in a while and I want you to phone your father to tell him that I'm going to drop you off in Coventry. I'm not taking you to Coventry but I want them to be expecting you elsewhere.'

'Okay.'

There was no radio or tape playing in the car so I knew straight away by the sound, as well as by the movement of the vehicle, when we began to slow down.

He stopped the car in what he said was a lay-by with a telephone.

'There are a couple of lorries parked here but it looks as if the drivers must be asleep. I think it's all right. Put the cardigan back over your head and I'll come round.'

During the short time it took him to walk around the back of the car and help me out of the passenger seat I was engulfed by fear. I knew that he had collected the ransom money and that everything had gone smoothly. The fact that he was here proved that. I also knew I was now superfluous to requirements. He said he was taking me home but I had no way of knowing that was the direction in which we were going. I didn't even know for sure we were in a lay-by or, if we were, whether both of us would be leaving it.

Without ever consciously allowing myself to acknowledge it, I had felt the workshop would be an unlikely place to murder me. Why would he run the risk of removing a dead body from what was clearly his place of work? He had now got the money and he had got me far away from the workshop. We had been travelling at speed for between half an hour and an hour; we could be anywhere. Why would he want me to make a call home anyway? Why take the risk at this stage of being spotted? I didn't want to leave the car to phone home or anything else. I just wanted us to keep driving, but I put the cardigan over my head and said nothing as he helped me from the passenger seat.

It was something of a surprise to realise that after only eight or ten steps we were in a telephone box.

'Pick up the receiver,' he instructed, guiding my hand to the telephone cradle.

I clenched the phone to my ear and heard him put a coin into the box. It dropped straight through and clanged into the metal receptacle below the phone. He attempted to put the coin into the machine again, and again and again.

'It must be broken,' he mumbled as he searched for a different coin, adding, 'Well that's funny, it was all right when I telephoned Kevin Watts earlier. We will have to find another box somewhere.'

We returned to the car and travelled a short distance in silence before he complained that he was unable to see through the headlights and again, he pulled over before doing a U-turn into what seemed like a quiet, open space, where the noise of traffic seemed muffled. It was clearly a more secluded place than the lay-by and my fears surfaced again.

I felt that Bob had grown to like me during the time he had kept me prisoner but by the way he spoke of his mate I believed he would kill me if he'd been instructed by him to do so. Maybe the lay-by had been too exposed or perhaps, momentarily, he had chickened out of murder but after driving a couple of miles had decided there was simply no alternative. Was this, I wondered, where they would find my body in the morning?

He went round to the back of the car and opened up the hatchback door. I could hear him rustling things about. I panicked as I heard paper being scrunched up and the thud of him moving something heavy from one place to another.

What is he looking for, what is he getting out? I asked myself over and over again. How I didn't rip the blindfold off my face at that moment I will never know. There is no doubt that his early warning that I must keep the blindfold on at all times and his repeated questioning each time he prepared to get me out of the bin, as to whether I had it in place, had left a strong impression. I was by now frankly terrified at the thought of seeing his face. I knew that if I did he would have all the excuse he needed to kill me.

I heard him walk around to the front of the car and begin to rub at the headlights, first on the driver's side, then on the passenger side.

'That's better,' he said with a laugh when he returned to the car. 'What a night!'

Perhaps the overwhelming feeling of panic that rose and then dispersed when he returned to the car made me feel able to confront the unconfrontable. I told him how scared I had been that he would not return and get me out of the bin, that I had been frightened he might have been involved in an accident and I would have been left there.

'I was so terrified I thought I would commit suicide,' I said.

'You needn't have worried. I wouldn't have let you die. I told you I had a letter in my wallet that said, "This is not a hoax. Stephanie Slater is held in blah, blah, blah," and the police would have found it if I had had an accident. Anyway, how could you commit suicide in there?'

'I was going to suffocate myself with the quilt, hold it tightly over my face until I passed out and then died from lack of oxygen,' I confessed.

'Impossible,' he said dismissively.

'Why?'

'It just is. You wouldn't be able to smother yourself. Even if you could have held your breath until you passed out, the minute you did you would release the pressure on the quilt and the oxygen would get through to you again. It's like trying to strangle yourself. It can't be done because you would keep coming round as soon as you started to breathe.'

His tone told me he thought it was a crazy idea and of course it was, but given the lack of tools for the job and the fact that I had never before contemplated suicide, it had seemed reasonable at the time.

We seemed to be driving on a motorway. Bob said there was hardly any traffic about and that the fog had lifted. We talked about weather patterns, including the sand in rainfall from the Sahara and predicting the cold front. He seemed quite knowledgeable about weather cycles and told me he was able to predict the weather, which I thought was a bit rich: I wondered why he hadn't predicted the fog? But of course I didn't mention that. I told him my favourite amazing fact that if a sports car travelled towards the planet Saturn at 100 miles an hour and didn't stop once, it would take 950 years for it to reach the planet.

He seemed to like that one and a short discussion on astronomy followed.

'It's not far now,' he told me at one point. 'I bet you can smell Birmingham, can't you?'

I laughed but was too excited by what he had said to formulate an intelligent reply.

'Where's the best place in Birmingham to live then? You'll know that, being an estate agent.'

'There are a lot of nice areas: Sutton Coldfield is very nice,' I responded, but I wasn't really interested in small talk by this stage.

'As you know I was going to drop you off at a telephone box or near a police station but I've decided to drive you as near home as I can. I don't want you stood about on a night like this. We don't want anybody getting hold of you, do we?'

Like somebody who will rape me and keep me prisoner in a box for eight days? The man was truly beyond belief. What could anyone possibly do to me now that would be worse than what he had already done? But he seemed oblivious to the irony of his words.

Almost as if he was trying to reassure me that everything would soon be back to normal and that he would get me home safely, he continually read out the road signs to me as we approached Birmingham. I thought it strange at the time. After he had been so careful, why was he helping me chart his route by effectively providing me with a countdown of the miles and turnings?

'We are going over Spaghetti Junction now,' he said, identifying the infamous junction in Birmingham where so many motorways converge that from above it just looks like a mass of cooked spaghetti.

'There's a turn-off here to Castle Bromwich.'

From that point on he informed me of every turn in the road he was taking, every set of traffic lights and the names of prominent shops along the route. I helped direct him from memory.

'What's in front of you?' I asked excitedly.

'The Scott Arms shopping centre,' he replied.

I could hardly contain myself. 'Oh great, turn right at the lights!'

'You can take your blindfold off,' he told me, 'but keep your eyes shut.'

'I will,' I promised, as I fumbled to remove the blindfold for, please God, the last time.

He mentioned the name of a firm of solicitors and I told him where to turn left and left again. Within moments we were approaching the top of my road.

'There should be a house down here with a "For Sale" board in the garden. That's the top of my road, you can drop me there.'

'Will you have far to go?'

'No, only a couple of hundred feet.'

The car pulled into the pavement and stopped. I sat there with my eyes closed and my heart in my mouth. Bob made his final speech:

'I'm sorry about all this. I want you to remember what I've said. None of this was your fault. Get back to your normal life as soon as possible. You may need counselling. I'm really sorry it had to be you. Now, I want you to lean and open the door, get out, take your coat, and stand there. Do not look back at the car. Wait until you hear the car go and then get off home.'

'Okay.' I tried to do as he had asked but I couldn't find the door catch. I felt him lean over and open it. All the time I kept my eyes tightly closed, terrified that I might catch a glimpse of him and blow everything.

'Give me a kiss then,' he said removing his hand from the door catch. I quickly turned and with repulsion granted his request. By this time I didn't care, I was so nearly home.

'Bye then,' he said.

I got out of the car and discovered my legs were very wobbly. I stood on the pavement with my coat in my arms and tried to push the car door shut before I felt it being pulled firmly closed by him.

'Bye.'

I heard the car drive away fairly quickly and when it was almost out of earshot I opened my eyes.

I couldn't focus on anything. All around me the street lamps were swirling and my legs could barely hold me up. I had intended to run like a bat out of hell for home but found I could only stumble along like a drunk. Fortunately, I knew where I was going: down the road, round the corner, into the garden and up to the front door.

I hurled myself at it, banging on the knocker and ringing the bell at the same time. Within seconds the door opened but I didn't recognise the man who was there. I began to think I was in an awful nightmare. I had never seen this man before in my life and yet this was our house. Suddenly, behind him I saw my Dad. He pushed the man out of the way, reached out and pulled me into the house in one fluid movement.

'Come in Bab, it's all right,' he repeated as he kissed me and rubbed my arms. 'It's all right Bab, you're home, it's all over now.'

'It's our Stephanie!' he yelled upstairs to where my mother was waiting. 'She's home!'

·10·

THE NEXT FEW hours passed in a blur of activity. Our house seemed to be full of people – policemen, policewomen, police surgeons – I had never seen so many comings and goings through our lounge in my life.

On the journey back Bob had asked me what I would do when I got home. I had told him that what I wanted most of all was a long, hot bath. Unfortunately, that was out of the question until the police surgeon arrived to take samples. I passed the time reeling off as much information as I could recall, drinking hot, sweet tea and eating lettuce sandwiches – my first 'meal' since my morning porridge seventeen hours before.

I think the police had problems believing all the information I was blurting out was genuine. They probably felt I wouldn't be in any fit state to help them at that hour of the morning, but in fact I was high on adrenalin or something. I wanted to get it all out while it was fresh and clear in my mind, particularly if it was something that might help them catch him before he got back to wherever it was he was going. I jabbered out all the details of his car I could remember: that it was small, a hatchback with wind-down windows and possibly, since I hadn't been aware of him changing gear, an automatic.

When the female police surgeon arrived I was asked to undress while standing on a sort of sheet in the middle of the lounge floor. Although the room had been cleared I felt horribly embarrassed because I knew I must smell dreadful, not having had a proper wash for eight days.

'I'm really sorry,' I said apologetically. 'I know I must smell really horrible.'

'It's all right,' she reassured me, removing my clothes and giving me my dressing gown to slip on. 'I'll be as fast as I can – I know you must want to get into a shower.'

She took samples of hair, samples scraped from beneath my finger and toenails, and swabs from my hands and feet. Before I had entered the room Detective Ellie Baker had asked if there had been any sexual contact between myself and my kidnapper. I shook my head determinedly and said there had not, so it was hardly surprising that the police did not feel it necessary to subject me to more intimate examinations.

Considerate as she was, the extent of the police surgeon's examination was just about as much as I could have stood. I was desperate to wash away the stink and grime of my eight days in captivity, and the thought of having to undergo any type of internal examination would have been the last straw. It was difficult enough to cope with the intimacy of being swabbed and scraped at, knowing how thoroughly unpleasant it must be for anyone forced to be near me.

'Okay, that's fine,' the police surgeon eventually said. 'You can go and have a bath or a shower now if you want.'

I looked around my bedroom. The room I had slept in almost every night of my life looked alien to me.

I stood in front of the bathroom mirror and dragged a hairbrush through my dirty, smelly, tatty hair, again and again. My eyes looked dull and lifeless. I loathed the image that I saw reflected in the mirror as I viciously tugged the brush through the matted mess on my head. I pulled and jerked, revelling in the pain I felt as handful upon handful of hair came out by the roots. I threw it into the wash basin in front of me and as I looked at it, dark against the pale porcelain, I remembered the hanks of hair I had seen in the bath at Turnberry Road after the fight with Bob.

Tears streamed down my face as I turned on the shower and stepped in. What was wrong with me? Why the hell was I crying now? It was all over, as my Dad had said. I was free, back with my parents and my cats in a home full of police, where neither Bob or his mate could harm me. I pinched the back of my hand, hard, as I realised I had been doing since the moment I arrived home. I could feel the pain, therefore I must be alive. Inconceivable as it seemed, I had survived.

I rubbed shampoo into my hair and covered every inch of my body with soap, which I then scrubbed with a nailbrush in an effort to remove all trace of the past eight days – every vestige of dirt, pain, anxiety, humiliation and guilt. After half an hour under near-scalding water, during which I scoured parts of my body until they bled, only the dirt and a hell of a lot of skin had disappeared.

As I sat in my bedroom in my pyjamas and a clean dressing gown the police surgeon came in to speak to me. She told me that although the police realised that having just got home the last thing I would want to do was leave, they strongly advised that I did. The press, she said, had been aware of the story since the day I was kidnapped but had cooperated fully in keeping it under wraps for my protection. However, now that I had been released they must be told, and it was likely that a pack of newsmen and women would be on the doorstep within a couple of hours at most.

It was the last thing I wanted to do but I could see the sense in what she was saying. Within half an hour, still dressed in my pyjamas and a dressing gown, I was with Mum and Dad in a police car on the way to the Priory, a private hospital only a few miles away.

At the Priory things started to come back into perspective, even though we were in a strange, unknown place in the middle of the night. I talked to various members of the police, including Donna Cooper who, I learned, had spent most of the time I had been in captivity with my Mum and Dad. Looking at her I felt that she, like me, had doubted that I would ever be released.

Unconsciously I continued pinching and scratching myself to make sure I was still able to feel some physical reaction, and it was already driving Mum mad. I couldn't explain then, and still can't adequately, what a source of comfort it was to feel pain. It wasn't a cry for help: on the contrary it was a purely personal, selfish if you like, act. I didn't want anyone to notice me doing it, but if I could feel pain it was a reassurance to me that I had survived. Perhaps it is some primeval thing that a psychiatrist could explain; I can't say anything other than it was essential to me at that time.

Eventually, Mum and Dad were given a double room and I had a single one next door. I didn't want to be on my own. I felt I would never want to be on my own again, but after being reassured that there would be a police guard outside the door all night I agreed. In retrospect it was probably for the best: had Mum come in with me that night I may never have slept alone again. In any event, there wasn't much time for sleeping.

I remember lying in bed, with the light out, marvelling at the pattern on the curtains. As the moon filtered through them I noticed water lilies and reeds. After all the bright lights that my eyes were having trouble adjusting to, it was a relief to be in semi-darkness. I realised my sight must be getting back to normal as I began to notice more and more detail in the curtains. Behind the reeds there were birds, and in the foreground tiny squiggles I couldn't identify as anything in particular. I was still trying to work out what they were as I drifted off to sleep.

·11·

BREAKFAST THE following morning was a very civilised affair. Mum and Dad came to my room, after I had been checked over by a doctor who pronounced me to be 'in good shape given the circumstances', and we chatted away about the missing days and how they had coped. Both of them were full of praise for the way the police had handled things.

Slowly, I was coming to terms with what had happened to me. Through no fault of my own I had been kidnapped and held against my will for eight days, most of it spent in a box. In exchange for a ransom I had been released. I knew that kidnapping was an unusual crime in Britain. Even more unusual, although I didn't dwell on it at the time, was the fact that I was released alive.

I later discovered that my case was unique. In the annals of modern British crime there are no incidents of 'successful' kidnap, i.e. where the victim is returned unharmed to their family in return for payment of a ransom. However, even with this knowledge, I was totally unprepared for the welter of press interest that already surrounded the case.

After breakfast with Mum and Dad I had a visit from

some of the police force top brass, the people from the West Midlands and Yorkshire forces who had pooled their resources to help get me released and who were now working on finding the man, or men, responsible for the crime. Led by Mr Williams and Mr Thomas, the police explained the extent to which the press had cooperated in keeping the story under wraps in the belief that publicity would endanger my life. They stressed that I was under no pressure to give a press conference immediately, that if I wasn't up to it they could postpone it. But, they added, it would have to be faced at some time in the fairly near future.

I was still on an adrenalin-induced high from the night before. That, combined with the physical effects of only two or three hours' sleep, made me feel capable of tackling anything. I was free now, surrounded by police: there was no way Bob or his mate could get to me here. I felt I could handle anything – so I agreed to speak to the press straight away. The doctor persuaded me to take a mild sedative before I left the Priory, which helped calm any feelings of nervousness that built up on the car journey to the Tally Ho police training centre in Birmingham for the press conference.

The police had explained that I would be fully debriefed, a process that would take days rather than hours, after the conference. They reminded me that the kidnapper was still at large and that I should be cautious in what I said. WPC Donna Cooper, who had spent much of the last week with Mum and Dad, would sit next to me at the press conference, and if there were any questions I didn't want to answer I should squeeze her hand and she would deflect them.

I realised that I had greatly underestimated public interest in the kidnap. While I was in captivity, listening to the hourly radio news bulletins, I had not been surprised that my disappearance was not mentioned. People go missing all the time, some never to be heard of again. It came as something of a surprise then that so many people had been aware of what was going on in my case but, in my interests, had agreed to a news blackout. However, nothing, but nothing, could have prepared me for the scores of reporters and the batteries of photographers and television cameramen that met my startled eyes when I walked into the room.

Mum and Dad were up on the stage with me and Donna Cooper as a sea of faces emerged, illuminated by flash after flash of light. Photographers scrambled about, jockeying for position. Above the whirring of the cameras, there was a roar of unintelligible conversation in the background. It reminded me of being under water in a crowded swimming pool – that strange disembodied sound you hear: a wall of noise you are not a part of until you break the surface and are able to distinguish individual words and voices. I gripped Donna Cooper's hand for dear life. I didn't want to answer any of their questions; what was I doing here?

'How do you feel to be free?'

'How did you feel when you were abducted?'

'Did you ever give up hope?'

'What was the worst part?'

The questions came thick and fast, not just to me but to Mum and Dad as well. Sometimes the police would intervene before I could reply. For the most part I answered the questions I felt comfortable with and squeezed Donna Cooper's hand if I felt there was a matter I didn't want to speak about or one that I should first discuss with the police.

I know now that some of the journalists felt let down. They believed that after cooperating with the police during the period of my incarceration they were entitled to more than the fairly anodyne responses they got that morning. Fortunately, I was completely oblivious to that at the time. To me it was a source of astonishment they were interested at all. Leaving the press conference in an unmarked police car, I saw a dozen or more huge vans, some with satellite dishes on the top, with the names of television stations emblazoned on their sides: Sky Television, BBC, GMTV, Central, even foreign stations I have never heard of. I couldn't believe it: all these people here, just for this.

The enormity of what had happened and the public reaction to it finally crystallised on my return to the Priory several hours later. Entering the reception area I saw a man reading a Birmingham evening newspaper. Almost the whole of the front page was covered by a picture of my face, with the banner headline announcing that I was free and alive.

The police debriefing back at the Priory in Edgbaston was sensitively handled but thorough. I went through every detail of the previous eight days, from before I arrived at 153 Turnberry Road on that Wednesday morning to the moment when Bob had driven away on the night he collected the ransom money and took me home. Except one. I never, in any conversation, either with my parents, with the police, or later with journalists, alluded to the rape.

When Detective Inspector Ellie Baker had asked me, the night I returned home, whether there had been any sexual contact between myself and the kidnapper, I had shaken my head and told her there hadn't been. I was never pressed on the point then or later. Over the course of the next few months, when the police had become an almost permanent fixture in my life, I frequently regretted my lie. But it was too late by then, or so I thought.

Almost immediately after my release I became aware of

press reports linking my kidnap with the abduction and subsequent murder of Julie Dart. I did not recall Julie's disappearance just a few months earlier. I think in those days I was a bit too preoccupied with myself and my own life to pay much attention to many of the stories that appeared in the news.

Eighteen-year-old Julie disappeared in the Leeds area in July. Three days after she failed to return home a handwritten letter was delivered to her boyfriend Dominic Murray. The note said Julie had been kidnapped. The letter was a desperate plea for help which Dominic and Julie's mother, Lynne Dart, responded to immediately by contacting the police.

Leeds police were not surprised: they too had received a letter that day, bearing a similar Huntingdon postmark to the note received by Dominic. The letter said that a young prostitute had been snatched from the city's Chapeltown area and it went on to demand a ransom from the police of £145,000. Once the money was received the victim would be released. However, the letter warned, if the demands were not met, the hostage would be killed.

Vice-squad officers made enquiries in Leeds red-light areas where a number of prostitutes said they recognised Julie's photograph. She had, they said, appeared in the area just a couple of weeks earlier to work alongside them. The police snapped into action immediately. Further correspondence from the kidnapper instructed a policewoman to await a call at a public telephone box on a platform at Birmingham's New Street railway station. The letter said the WPC would be told to follow instructions which would lead her to a series of telephone boxes. At each stop she should collect further instructions. Other specific information, including details of how the ransom money should be packaged, the used notes it must contain and a final warning that should anything go wrong the hostage would never be seen alive again, were also contained in the misspelled handwritten message. It also threatened that a large city centre store would be firebombed.

Despite the best efforts of the police, ten days after her disappearance Julie Dart's body was discovered in a field near Grantham in Lincolnshire, near a disused railway line known as the Ironstone Quarry Line. Her decomposing remains were wrapped in a sheet and tied with cord. She appeared to have been battered to death.

While I was still at the Priory hospital undergoing debriefing the name of Julie Dart came up several times on radio and television news items. Julie was also mentioned at the press conference I had given, but at that time her name meant nothing to me. I had no idea of any possible link between the two crimes. The police said almost nothing about Julie's case although it now seems clear that they were fairly sure, even while I was still in captivity, that the same person was responsible for both crimes, as well as extortion threats to British Rail. After what had happened to Julie, they must have realised the chances of me ever being seen alive again were remote but I was still blissfully unaware of it.

Sitting in my bedroom at the Priory watching the news on television, I saw Lynne Dart, Julie's mother, being interviewed. It was only then that I realised that the police, the press, everyone but me had made the connection. Lines of worry were etched on her face. Her only daughter had been kidnapped and murdered and until the man responsible was found and brought to justice she would not be able to rest, she said. I watched enthralled as she was interviewed and was genuinely shocked by what I saw. Was it possible, I asked myself, that Bob could be responsible for the death of this woman's daughter?

I remembered his face as he attacked me in the bathroom at Turnberry Road, how his mouth had been contorted with rage. That image was virtually the last one I saw before he blindfolded me. All the time I was in the workshop, in the box or outside it, I retained that picture of him in my mind's eye. It was the last picture I focused on before eight days of darkness, and there were many times when I truly believed it was the last real image I would ever see. I thought of his horrible coldness as he forced me to lie on the mattress before he raped me, and shuddered. And yet he had also shown me moments of kindness, we had talked and occasionally even laughed together. Was it possible that the man who had rubbed my stiff and aching elbows that first morning, when I was too sore to move after my first night in the box, could be responsible for battering a teenager to death?

'Now that Stephanie Slater has been released, do you feel she may be able to help you learn more about the man who murdered your daughter, Mrs Dart?' the television journalist asked.

Lynne Dart looked straight into the camera and said in a carefully measured voice with a strong northern accent: 'I'm relying on her, I'm relying on her to tell the police everything she knows.'

As I sat on the bed, continuing to stare at the television news, I was hit by the full impact of my very narrow escape, and I burst into tears. Since my release I hadn't been able to cry. Now it seemed I would not be able to stop. There were tears of sorrow for Julie Dart and her family, tears of anger about what had happened to me and of fear so long repressed, but most of all there were tears of relief, relief that I was alive and safe. If it was true, that Bob had killed Julie Dart, if it was true he had battered her senseless, then why hadn't he done the same to me? How had I escaped when she had not? I recalled how I had felt during my eight days of captivity and wondered if Julie had experienced similar emotions: the terror of entering the dark, cold workshop, that first night; the pain of being bound hand and foot and locked in the box. The poor kid was just eighteen years old. It wasn't fair, any of it. I continued to sob until my tears ran out.

I discovered that Shipways' personnel department was being inundated with media requests for my exclusive story. One of their employees, Mervyn Measures, was assigned to the task of sorting through the offers and presenting them to me. The police told me that if I signed with one of the newspapers exclusively, I would be taken under that paper's wing and the others would stop bombarding me with requests for photographs and interviews. All the national papers I had ever heard of seemed to be interested in the story. The amounts of money being offered left me speechless: to me they represented a fortune. I had absolutely no idea how to handle the requests or make an informed decision so, at Mervyn Measures' suggestion, I put the matter in the hands of an agent in Scotland called Jack Irvine. Jack negotiated with the tabloids and eventually I signed a contract with the *Sun*.

Financially, the *Sun* was offering the most lucrative deal but there were other reasons why I favoured it. My Dad reads it, he always has, so I felt I was more familiar with it than any other newspaper. I also knew it had a high circulation and if I was going to tell my story I wanted to tell it to the largest possible audience.

I felt then, as I do now, that women are very exposed and vulnerable in some jobs and I wanted this subject aired in the papers. Because it would be expensive or time-consuming to introduce safety measures, women continue to be at risk. Carrying a mobile telephone might have saved me from being kidnapped from Turnberry Road. All it would have taken was for Shipways to operate a procedure where their agents called in to the office before entering a property and again when viewing was complete – a procedure that should never take longer than twenty or thirty minutes. Having a mobile telephone might not have stopped Bob taking me prisoner, but by 11 am Shipways could have known there was something wrong. In the event, it was ages before the police were finally informed. And that was only after Bob had contacted Kevin Watts. In the meantime I was on my way to the workshop.

In the days following my release my time was divided between answering questions for the police and giving interviews to the *Sun*. I feel sure that the activity helped me at that time. I didn't want the opportunity to sit down and think about what had happened to me. I wanted to be on the move.

The *Sun* whisked me to a series of posh hotels where I tried to provide them with material for a serialised story; the police were busy setting up re-enactments of the possible routes I may have travelled to the workshop, or anything that might throw new light on events. Travelling in a hatchback car from Turnberry Road, they drove me for miles through built-up areas asking if I could recall stopping at this or that set of traffic lights. In order to help them as much as possible I sat, partially reclined and with my eyes closed, trying to recall if one stop felt more familiar than another. I'm not sure whether my efforts aided them but I was more than happy to continue if there was any possibility that they might.

One day we travelled for miles, up towards Manchester and the Peak District. We stopped in a lay-by and they asked me if it felt like the one Bob and I stopped at on the night he brought me home. I thought I would never forget how I had felt as I stood waiting and praying that the coin Bob kept feeding into the machine would work or that he would tire of fiddling with it. But as I

147

stood facing the telephone handset with my eyes closed I couldn't remember if this had been the way I was standing on that night. Already my memory was beginning to dull and I knew that time was against me in trying to recall anything that might provide some clue as to where I had been and the person responsible for taking me there.

In an attempt to keep me well away from any other newspapers, to ensure their story remained as exclusive as possible, the *Sun* wanted to foot the bill to send me and a couple of journalists on a foreign holiday. The Bahamas was one destination mentioned. I was adamant: I didn't want to leave Britain. Even the suggestion of travelling to France was too much for me, and I burst into tears when it was suggested. I had been taken away and held against my will once; I wasn't about to let it happen again.

Meanwhile, all the newspapers seemed to be united in campaigning for Bob's early capture. Under headlines calling him 'the most wanted man in Britain' Bob's face, as I recalled it, stared out from every tabloid newspaper in the country, following the release of a description and a photofit likeness I had worked on with the police.

Although they continued to work together, relations between the press and the police were far from harmonious. The general press feeling seemed to be that the police had made a cock-up of arresting the kidnapper on the night the ransom had been paid. Apparently, over a thousand police personnel had been involved in the operation and yet the kidnapper had still been able to collect the ransom money, escape and, almost adding insult to injury, been able to drop me within a few hundred feet of my front door, without attracting the attention of one of them. Some fairly harsh comments were made in the newspapers.

I think certain national newspaper journalists were also peeved at the way things had been handled after my release. The timing of the press conference meant that while television and radio stations and mainly regional evening papers were able to make front-page news of the fact I had been released alive, the national newspaper reporters who had shown such forbearance in not breaking the story while my whereabouts were unknown found themselves looking for a new angle on what was fast becoming old news.

Naturally I was fascinated to learn of the events of that final night, when I lay in the workshop cooped up in the cold, airless box, wondering if Bob would ever return.

It seems that Kevin Watts had been issued with a set of instructions, read to him over the telephone at Shipways' Great Barr office. He set out in his own car from Birmingham, travelling alone through Staffordshire and Cheshire, skirting Greater Manchester before entering Derbyshire, where he had been told to await a telephone call at a pay phone in Glossop railway station.

Hampered by the fog, Kevin was over an hour late at Glossop station but the kidnapper had made allowances, or had been watching his progress, because he eventually received the call which directed him to a series of public telephone boxes where instructions had been taped beneath the telephone directory shelf. By following these instructions Kevin progressed ever nearer his goal. Each time he returned to his car he would read the contents of the written messages aloud, enabling the police, who had previously installed a two-way listening device in his car, to chart his every move.

Hours after leaving Birmingham, Kevin found himself in an area completely unknown to him, over the Pennines in Dodworth, close to the Dove Valley Trail, a disused former railway line, the site selected by the kidnapper for the ransom drop.

The original intention had been for the police to shadow Kevin Watts in a series of unmarked cars, maintaining radio contact with him throughout. Immediately following the drop, the suspect would be picked up. At least that had been the plan. What had in fact happened was that in the appalling weather conditions, unknown to Kevin, radio contact between his car and the police broke down. The police had lost sight of his car and were unaware of what was going on as he made the drop. He was completely on his own as, following instructions, he turned into a lonely, dark bridle path. A makeshift Shipways sign told him he was on the right route.

Only a few yards further along his headlights picked out a new set of instructions fastened to a red and white traffic cone in the middle of the path. Doing exactly as the message said, he removed the money from the bag it was in and placed it on an open wooden drawer balanced on the parapet of a bridge spanning the Dove Valley Trail below. He then returned to his car and drove back in the direction he had come.

Hearing Kevin's car disappear into the distance Bob and his mate must have pulled the drawer off the bridge with a length of washing line attached to its handle, gathered up the cash and been off down the disused railway line before the police were able to get a fix on what was going on. Thus, they managed to get away with £175,000 in cash.

Although the money had not been bugged, the serial number of each note had been recorded on video film. Unfortunately, according to press reports at the time, the video film was later lost, making the ransom money untraceable. Whether this was true or not, the press had a field day at the expense of the police.

For the most part I was unaware of all this conflict. The *Sun*, which, because of my exclusivity contract, was the only newspaper I was talking to, didn't seem to have any gripe with the police; but then having access to me, they could afford to approach the story from an entirely different angle. They had finally realised I was not prepared to travel abroad so agreed to set up a photo-shoot in the Isle of Wight. I felt sorry for the journalists and photographers who thought they would be heading off for a mid-February assignment in the Bahamas but since the *Sun* was determined I could not remain free of rival press attention if I stayed in Birmingham, the Isle of Wight was the only place I wanted to be.

·12·

W E ALL HAVE a place we consider our own personal heaven on earth. To some it may be a secluded beach on a sun soaked island in the south seas, to others the bottom of their own back garden or the vegetable patch of their allotment. Mine is the Isle of Wight.

Many of my friends set great store by saving up all year to strike out for their two-week annual holiday in some exciting, unknown destination and, while I love hearing about their experiences and adventures, I have never envied them. I have been to Spain a couple of times with my parents but I wasn't greatly impressed. Lying in the sun all day isn't my idea of a good time and frankly I spent most of my time there wishing I was on the Isle of Wight. Give me the sight of the sea from St Catherine's Point, the majesty of Carisbrooke Castle, the Old Cider Barn at Godshill and I couldn't be happier.

As a child and later as a teenager I spent wonderful annual holidays on the island with Mum and Dad. Perhaps the excitement as we sat around the kitchen table every February planning for our two weeks in summer, or the warmth of the island people, for whom nothing seems too much trouble, or the wonderful feeling of being a child, tired after a busy day at the beach, feeling warm and safe tucked up in a hotel bedroom knowing your Mum and Dad are in the same room, have stayed with me longer than most.

I know a lot of people consider it crazy but it doesn't worry me in the slightest. Even the Red Funnel ferry that travels to and fro from the mainland every half hour remains something almost magical as far as I'm concerned. So it was with enormous joy that I found myself heading out of Southampton towards Cowes, with a bevy of journalists from the *Sun* and several police officers in tow.

We stayed in the Shanklin Manor Hotel where the owners kindly allowed us use of their private facilities, including a swimming pool, sauna and pool room. A close friend from home, whom I first telephoned from the Priory hospital when I was released, joined me for the trip. Lisa had been a friend for years: we had more or less grown up together, and her presence was a great comfort to me at that time. When I wanted to talk she listened, and if I didn't that was okay too. The experience of being surrounded by press and police could have been a daunting one but having Lisa around made it all so much more normal.

I was being interviewed and photographed for several hours a day but when the work was over we all relaxed together over a meal and a drink. Evenings took on a private party atmosphere, because there were so many of us. But if Lisa and I chose to miss out on an evening's entertainment to enjoy a bowl of soup in our room while watching television, no one objected.

A couple of days after arriving on the island, I was walking by the sea front at Ventnor, one of my favourite spots. Suddenly, from the open door of a café I heard a sound that made my blood run cold. I stood stock still and clenched my fists as I tried to keep down a mounting feeling of terror.

I stood staring wildly at the almost empty road, where only a couple of local people were going about their business thirty or forty yards away. I pulled myself together and started to walk back in the direction from which we had come. The sound that had struck such fear into my heart had been nothing more than a radio jingle. It just happened to be the jingle played immediately before the hourly news bulletin on Radio Two. For an awful moment the memory of the scores of times I had lain in the box listening to that music came flooding back to me.

That evening, still in Ventnor, a group of us, Lisa, myself, journalists and police, visited the Spyglass Inn, a favourite pub of mine with a lot of unusual, dark little rooms and a wonderful large paved balcony area outside, with uninterrupted views of the sea. After the meal I took the WPC who had spent hours with me since my release to one side.

'I'm just going to go out on the balcony,' I said quietly.

She looked alarmed. There were several tables and chairs out on the balcony but not a soul in sight.

'Wait a minute, I'll come with you,' she said looking round for her coat.

'No, don't. Please. I just want to go out for a minute on my own. I'll be all right.'

Reluctantly, she agreed, but as I opened the door to step outside, every copper in the place pulled their chair towards the window to keep a wary eye on me.

I stood outside, pulling my big black coat around me to keep out the chill of the mid-February night. Only yards away I could hear the sea crashing against the rocks below the balcony. The beam from the lighthouse at St Catherine's Point swept over the water and disappeared, and I could see the lights of distant ships, somewhere miles away, between me and the French coast of Normandy. On board those ships were people I would never know and they would never know me, but for tonight we were all part of the same picture. Looking across the deserted beach I saw white-topped waves run up the sand, before returning to the mighty body of water behind them. It was a wonderful moment. I was freezing cold but I felt young and alive. The cobwebs of the workshop had finally been blown away and as I stood there I felt as free and as strong as the wind that whipped my hair over my eyes or the waves breaking on the rocks below.

Even in February on the sleepy Isle of Wight, it was impossible to escape from events completely. The BBC television programme *Crimewatch* was scheduled to present an edition on my kidnap two nights before we were due to leave the island. The police and journalists with me had mentioned that taped messages received from the kidnapper would be played in the hope that somebody would recognise his voice. Another important piece of information had also emerged in recent days. A man named Purvis Barnaby had been looking out of an upstairs window the night Bob drove me home to Birmingham. Bob had parked right under a street light and Mr Barnaby had recognised the vehicle I got out of as an old-style Metro. Because he was a professional paint-sprayer Mr Barnaby could say with conviction that the car was vermilion red in colour.

His recollections of the evening were clear. He remembered that as I got out of the passenger door I had been unsteady on my feet. When Bob drove off into the night and I finally opened my eyes, after eight days in darkness I was unable to see, everything was a swirling blur, illuminated by street lights. I stumbled and reeled and Mr Barnaby, not surprisingly given that it was the early hours of the morning, thought I was drunk.

I didn't want to be with the police and journalists when the *Crimewatch* programme was on. They were a great crowd but at the end of the day this was just part of their job, whereas it was part of my life. At the Priory the police had played a tape of a message received by Shipways during my captivity. Unannounced, one of the policewomen had turned on a hand-held machine, and suddenly Bob's voice was in the room with us. I could see the logic behind springing his voice on me but I was completely traumatised by the action and felt nervous and jittery for a couple of hours afterwards.

However, here I felt safe with the police around me because I knew there was no way Bob could get past them. Actually, it wasn't Bob that frightened me, it was his mate. I was terrified he would want to shut me up to prevent me being able to identify them and, from what Bob had said, if that was his plan he would find some way of achieving it. The thought that I had never seen this man, never even heard his voice, compounded my fear. I could be in the same room with him and not know it. He could have been anyone: the man behind me in the paper shop or a waiter at the hotel. The thought terrified me. I realise now that the whole idea was fanciful but at the time my worries seemed justified, particularly since the police who accompanied me to the island were so reluctant to let me out of their sight.

I decided that if I had the same reaction to Bob's voice when I heard it on *Crimewatch* I would rather be away from the others so Lisa and I said we would watch the programme on the television in our room.

It was an unnerving experience but this time I was prepared for it. Bob had made no attempt to disguise his voice, which seemed strange. Surely, he must have considered the possibility that his instructions to Kevin would be recorded? There was no doubt at all that it was him and I wondered fleetingly if someone else out there was sitting watching the programme and thinking the self-same thing. There must be a mother, father, sister, brother, wife, child or friend to whom that voice was familiar. Surely, someone, somewhere could come forward with a name.

I was sorry my time on the island was coming to an end but the journalists had completed their interviews, the photographers had masses of pictures and the police who had accompanied us were keen to get back to their families on the mainland. Even Lisa was, I felt, about ready to pick up the threads of her normal life again, and I didn't blame her. She had been a tower of strength but she had a job, a family and other friends back in Birmingham that she naturally wanted to see. For myself, I could have stayed on there for ever. The day before we were due to leave a small group of us decided to visit Carisbrooke Castle, while the others had a look around Newport. The castle is a wonderful old place, steeped in history. It stands majestically at the top of a hill near Newport. From its ramparts on a clear day it is possible to imagine one can see over to France, from where its architects, the Normans, originated.

As Lisa and I strolled about it seemed as if we had Carisbrooke to ourselves. Although the castle is one of only a very few attractions open to winter tourists, the place was deserted. To one side of the courtyard I could see our crowd huddled together having a chat.

'What will you do when you go home?' asked Lisa.

'What do you mean?'

'Will you go back to work, back to Shipways?'

'I don't know, I haven't really thought about it. I suppose so.'

'What about David?'

'What about him?'

'Will you keep seeing him?'

'I expect so, why not?'

'I just wondered,' she replied with a shrug.

I think Lisa had probably grasped a fundamental question that I was still nowhere near to understanding. The kidnap itself may have taken only eight physical days out of my life, time which, if I chose, I could sit and calculate in terms of hours, minutes and even seconds. But after the events of those eight days would life, as I had known it, ever be the same again? At the end of it all would it be more like eight months or eight years I had been robbed of? That day at Carisbrooke I really believed it was just a matter of time. The jigsaw of my life had been kicked off the table but, as far as I was concerned, all the pieces were there; it was just a matter of putting them back together again.

As we walked through the courtyard, Gordon, one of the policemen in the group, broke away and came towards us smiling.

'You're in demand, you are,' he said nodding towards me.

'What do you mean, what have I done?'

'There's a lot of people been trying to get hold of you,' he said.

I laughed. 'Oh, blimey!' I immediately thought that some tabloid journalists must have discovered our whereabouts. The *Sun* reporters had been paranoid ever since our arrival that we were being trailed by journalists from other papers. To listen to them, every tree on the island might conceal a newspaperman from a rival paper. Lisa and I, with no previous experience of the national press, had come to regard it as a bit of a joke. We reckoned the secret service probably had nothing on the men and women of Fleet Street when it came to subterfuge and suspicion.

'Come over to the car and get in,' he said, leading me towards an unmarked police car parked just outside the massive gates of Carisbrooke Castle. I got into the back seat of the car with Lisa, Gordon sat in the front.

Turning to look at me, his face serious now, he said, 'I've got some news for you, Steph. They've picked him up. We've got him.'

I sat in silence, clutching Lisa's hand. 'Thank God,' I whispered and I meant it.

The remainder of the day was a complete farce. From enjoying a fairly free and easy time we were suddenly thrown into the middle of a three-ring media circus. The *Sun* photographer, Gary Stones, was like a dog with two tails, chasing about taking pictures of me reading the paper in a variety of locations, including a television shop in the High Street, where he managed to persuade the manager to put a chair and a television set at our disposal. I sat watching a kids' cartoon as Gary shot off a roll of film. The idea, he explained, was that a picture of the kidnapper would later be superimposed on to the television screen I was watching. After that we made a mad dash for the ferry across the island in the police car. We were late so with blue lights flashing we raced towards the terminal at Cowes where the ferry was still in: the captain had been asked to wait for us.

To avoid any confrontations with newspaper reporters I sat up with the captain on the way back to the mainland – another photo-opportunity for Gary who, I was convinced, saw rival photographers in his sleep. However, his suspicions were confirmed as the ferry pulled into Southampton and a dozen or more journalists and photographers could be seen scanning every vehicle that left the boat. I didn't see them, I was lying in the back of the car with a blanket over me but somehow they were aware of our arrival. We set off towards Birmingham in an unmarked police car but after only a few miles the driver was forced to clamp a flashing blue light on to the roof of it. Eventually we lost them.

On the drive home I learned more about the man who had kidnapped me. His name was not Bob but Michael, Michael Benniman Sams. After the *Crimewatch* programme describing his old, vermilion-red Metro and broadcasting the tape of his voice, the police enquiry room had been inundated with calls. However, a lead supplied by a Yorkshire woman, Mrs Susan Oake, claiming the voice and car belonged to her ex-husband, had paid off. Mrs Oake had seen her ex-husband only days earlier at a family funeral and thought then that he and his car matched the description of the wanted man. However, until she heard the kidnapper's voice on *Crimewatch*, which because of her suspicions she had videoed, she couldn't be sure. Even with the evidence of his appearance and his car, Mrs Oakes felt one major detail, that would have incriminated her ex-husband beyond doubt, was missing. It was the fact that he had only one leg.

Police officers working on the case visited Sams' home, a detached white house in Sutton-on-Trent in Nottinghamshire, the following day. His current wife, Teena, told the police that her husband had said they might call, after the *Crimewatch* programme which they had watched together mentioned an old vermilion-red Metro. Teena Sams directed police to her husband's workshop eight miles away.

Arriving at T&M Tools, a workshop in Swan and Salmon Yard at Castlegate, Newark, the police were convinced they had found their man. The man they met there fitted the description of Bob but even more convincing was the fact that his radio was tuned to Radio Two and the workshop, including the telephone, the microwave, and the beamed ceiling, was exactly as I had described it in my statement.

·13·

MORE THAN FIFTEEN months were to pass before Michael Sams was brought to trial. During that time the police amassed vital information linking him with the murder of Julie Dart and also with attempts to extort money from British Rail. Most of the ransom money paid for my release was also discovered by following up leads Sams inadvertently gave the police himself, while trying to outwit them.

It was a strange period of time for me. In the weeks after Sams' arrest I was still very involved with the press and with the police, who continued to offer a great deal of support and kept me up to date with developments as they came to light. Public interest in the case didn't evaporate immediately Sams was arrested, as I had anticipated. Shortly after being taken into custody, he confessed to kidnapping me but continued to deny responsibility for Julie's death. The police were convinced he was lying from the outset.

Soon after he was arrested, at a meeting in Leeds, I met Julie Dart's mother and grandparents. They were lovely warm people with a strong sense of family: it was evident that Julie had been a much loved girl. She sometimes spent an evening at the pub with her Mum, and it was evident that they had been real friends as well as mother and daughter. Though money might have been tight at times, there was obviously no shortage of love and affection.

I have since been asked whether I feel I was exploited by the media during those weeks. I didn't feel that at all. I don't dispute that my meeting with Lynne Dart presented a unique 'photo opportunity', especially when I went with her to put flowers on Julie's grave. But I wanted to meet Lynne Dart and would have tried to do so with or without the encouragement of the press.

There is a part of me that still finds it difficult to come to terms with the fact that I survived and Julie didn't. Unlike Lynne, my parents didn't have to live with the knowledge that their daughter had been taken away, violently murdered and her body dumped in a field. God knows, they went through enough, but at least they were spared that. When I met Lynne in a hotel in Leeds, her first words to me were:

'Did he mention our Julie?'

He hadn't, and I told her so, but I was glad to be able to reassure her that I would do everything in my power to help the police discover any similarities that might exist in the two cases. If Sams was responsible for Julie's murder, her family had the right to know. As it stood Lynne didn't even know the date of her daughter's death. Between her disappearance and the discovery of her body more than a week later, nothing was known.

I was also asked whether I thought Sams had murdered Julie. Despite the welter of evidence that continued to build up against him over the months before the trial, I would shake my head and say I didn't know and that I didn't like to think about it.

It was true that I didn't like to think about it but that

didn't stop me doing so. Not a day, maybe not even an hour passed that something would happen to jerk me back to the time spent in the workshop and I would wonder again if Julie had also been kept prisoner there. It is sometimes impossible to block thoughts out – I had found that to my cost during my final hours in the box. But however much you may not want to confront them they keep pushing and shoving their way to the very front of your mind and nothing can shift them.

I was living in a strange twilight world back with Mum and Dad, sleeping into the afternoon, talking to friends who came round to the house to see me in the evening, then watching videos and drinking wine long into the night. Mum and Dad did everything they could to help me through the anguish but they are ordinary working people with no knowledge of how to deal with that sort of thing.

I had consistently refused offers of psychiatric help. One part of me thought I was strong enough to cope, to get through it on my own without professional help. That was what I told anyone who asked. But another part dreaded the thought of starting to peel back the layers; I didn't want to start opening up and exposing myself. If I started to talk I might not stop, and there were things I didn't want anyone to know.

Every day when I woke, before even opening my eyes, I was immediately aware of a huge cloud of anxiety pressing down on me. Often a few seconds would elapse before I was sufficiently awake to identify what it was, but it was always there. That oppressive, anxious feeling became as familiar to me as my own face in the mirror; it was with me every minute of every day. Sometimes, if I was talking to people or watching something funny on television it would retreat a little bit, but it never disappeared entirely.

I raged against my inability to 'pull myself together'. It

didn't make it any easier to keep reading in the newspapers about what a hero I was, although in some ways I know I fostered that belief. I just couldn't seem to stop putting on a brave face. I think that after all the hullabaloo that had surrounded my release I didn't want to let everyone down. I wanted things to be back to normal, I wanted the story to have a happy ending. Only those closest to me knew that I was falling apart.

About a month after my release a couple of men from Shipways' head office came to visit me at home. I didn't know either of them but they seemed pleasant enough. They said how dreadful the experience must have been for me and how they hoped I was back on the road to recovery. Neither of them mentioned me returning to work although they said the house market seemed to be picking up and that my colleagues at the Great Barr office were very busy. I didn't think much of it at the time.

A short while later I had a personal letter from one of Shipways' directors. Again, it was very sympathetic and supportive and again it mentioned how very busy my colleagues at the Great Barr office were. Suddenly, the penny dropped. 'Oh God, they want me to go back to work,' I said out loud. I was so preoccupied with other things I can honestly say that I hadn't given the idea a thought. I didn't mention the letter but for a couple of days I turned the idea over in my mind, then I talked to Mum and Dad. 'I think I'm going to try to go back to work,' I told them.

When I arrived at the office on my first day back, press and photographers were three deep outside the window. After Kevin Watts and I had posed for several pictures and I had announced how glad I was to be back they left, but for the entire day the office was inundated with people coming in under the pretext of picking up a property guide. Others didn't bother with an excuse, they would just come and press their faces against the window in twos and threes. When one of them had worked out which one I was they would point me out to their friends. It was a horrible experience, like being in a goldfish bowl.

During the course of the day I had a long chat with Kevin, who had so bravely driven for hours, alone through the fog, to deliver the ransom money for my release. He is a smashing bloke who tried his very best to help me feel at ease, but throughout the day I was shaking like a leaf. Every time the phone rang I jumped and wondered who it might be. I knew it couldn't be Sams but his familiarity with Shipways was an unnerving factor, and it was only by a gargantuan effort I found myself there to face day two.

On the second day Kevin took me out with him on a couple of valuation jobs. Perhaps he hoped to revitalise some of the old enthusiasm – but it was hopeless, and so was I. That night I tried to give myself a good talking to. I knew that if I was going to stay at Shipways I was just going to have to buckle down and deal with things. People would eventually get tired of staring and pointing me out. I knew they didn't mean to be unkind and I resolved to try to shrug it off if I could.

The next day I set off with a more positive attitude. There was still a lot of activity in the shop, with people calling in all the time to see if I was about. If for some reason I was in the back of the office, they would hang around reading house details until I put in an appearance. I did try to laugh it off but it didn't work.

At lunch-time I wanted to go to West Bromwich to buy a telescope. Since my release I found I had a lot more hours to spend looking at the night sky; though I had tried to resume my old social life with my mates at the Malt

Shovel it hadn't really worked. After a couple of times when I just felt like a public spectacle, I decided to stay at home.

I asked Kevin if someone could be spared to come with me to the shop. I was still very nervous of being alone for any length of time unless I was in the car. He agreed to let Richard, a young lad who had only recently started work, come with me. We bought the telescope and took it back to the office. I was feeling quite cheerful, looking forward to the end of the day when I could get home and assemble it.

It was about 4 pm and unusually there were just two of us in the office, Richard and myself. I was fiddling about with some new house details that had come in, looking through the filing cabinet for properties of similar size and price, when a cup of coffee that had been left on top of the filing cabinet hours earlier shook as I pulled out a drawer, and fell spilling its contents all over me.

'Oh no!' I yelled as I ran towards the kitchen to sponge out the stain. As I was dabbing at the material with cold water I looked into the mirror above the sink and was surprised to see tears streaming down my face. That was it, the floodgates opened, I cried and cried and to this day, I don't know what it was all about. Poor Richard must have thought I was crackers. He came into the kitchen to see if I had managed to get my dress clean and found me a gibbering wreck. He was full of concern.

'Are you all right?' he kept asking me in a worried little voice.

'Look, I think I had better go home,' I told him. 'Will you be okay here on your own?'

'Yes, course I will. Kevin will be back soon, anyway,' he reassured me.

With that I just grabbed my coat and bag and ran, out of the shop, across the busy road to the car park where I got into my car, locked the doors and, for the first time since my release, I cried as if I would never stop. I must have sat there for about ten or fifteen minutes. I just couldn't stop crying. When I eventually arrived home my Dad met me on the step. 'Are you all right, Bab?' he asked, opening his arms.

'I can't do it, Dad, I can't,' I choked out between sobs.

'I know you can't, Bab,' he said, pulling me to his chest. 'It doesn't matter.'

Shortly after that I began having strange dreams, all of them preoccupied with death and bodies. One night I awoke bathed in perspiration after having dreamed I was walking through a field towards a broken down old shack. I looked into the shack and saw a coffin in the corner. The wood of the coffin was shiny and new compared to the weathered and broken old boards of the shack that housed it. Something compelled me to walk towards the coffin and when I did I saw my own name on a silver plate screwed into the lid: Stephanie Slater, I read before turning and running like a bat out of hell back the way I had come. But now, instead of being in a field, I was running through a graveyard where skeletal hands and arms poked up through the earth.

The dreams were so terrifying I actually tried not to go to sleep at night. I would prop myself up in bed and watch television and drink wine until finally sleep would over-take me. But however long I managed to fend off sleep, the dreams always seemed to be there waiting.

I talked to my friends about the dreams. Lisa, Stacey and Danielle were coming to see me on an almost daily basis but our relationships had altered. I was no longer the life and soul of the party. I didn't want to go out, preferring to stay at home well away from what I thought were prying eyes.

My relationship with David had petered out through

apathy and neglect. We had tried to pick up where we left off but it was useless. I wasn't the same person any more and nobody was better aware of it than me. Lisa had met someone and, understandably, wanted to spend time with him, so it was to Danielle and Stacey that I turned with my problems about bad dreams. Both of them seemed to think that once the trial was over they would disappear.

I was pinning all my hopes on the trial by this stage. Once that was over, things surely would get back to normal.

·14·

T HE TRIAL OF Michael Sams opened on Wednesday 9 June 1993 at Nottingham Crown Court. It was not certain that I would be called to give evidence, since he had pleaded guilty to kidnapping me and blackmailing Shipways for the ransom, soon after being arrested. However, he continued to plead not guilty to charges relating to the kidnap and murder of Julie Dart and the attempt to blackmail Leeds City Police out of £145,000 for her release. He was charged with an additional blackmail attempt against Leeds police and an attempt to blackmail British Rail out of £200,000 by threatening to derail a passenger train.

As the trial date drew nearer I was told I would be called to give an account of what had happened to me. This, I was informed, would be presented as similar fact evidence in the case against Sams.

Similar fact evidence is only called when there is something particularly singular about the method used to carry out a crime. The police explained to me that Michael Sams' *modus operandi* in my case and that of Julie Dart had been remarkably similar and what they sought to bring to the attention of the jury were the hallmarks common to both.

I had heard that the police felt they had put together a very strong case but I had also been warned that once in court, anything can happen. I had never been in a court-room of any kind so the police arranged a visit to our local crown court. The case I saw being tried from the public gallery that day was not in any way similar to the one I would give evidence in but I learned who was the defence barrister, where the prosecution barrister sat and got some idea of general crown court practice. It was intended to make my task at Nottingham less daunting, but it didn't. When I was called into court I was shaking like a leaf.

By then the jury of eight women and four men had already been addressed by the prosecution barrister, Richard Wakerley QC, whose task it was to prove the case against Michael Sams.

I was told how, for two and a half days, Mr Wakerley had held the courtroom enthralled as he detailed how Sams plotted and schemed to commit the perfect crime. He described how he snatched Julie from Leeds and took her to Newark where he murdered her. Mr Wakerley talked of how Leeds City Police had made every effort to meet Sams' demands in order to save Julie's life but how because of a series of accidents and bungles, the ransom run had to be aborted. In response to a written request to their city centre headquarters, Leeds police placed an advertisement in the personal column of the *Sun*. 'Let's try again for Julie's sake,' it read, although eighteen-year-old Julie Dart was already dead by the time it appeared. The jury were also told of the threat to derail an express passenger train made to British Rail and the discovery of a device beneath the railway bridge at Millmeece, which had been used as a prop in the BR blackmail attempt and was probably constructed by Sams.

In the months between Sams' arrest and his court

appearance the police had worked tirelessly to build their case. After Susan Oake heard Sams' voice on *Crimewatch* they immediately went into action. When Sams was taken into custody a team of forensic scientists examined the workshop in minute detail. They discovered a number of important clues. As well as a stack of very unusual blue-coloured bricks outside the workshop which exactly matched one used by the blackmailer to anchor down a written demand, left on the hard shoulder of a motorway in his extortion attempt, the forensic team found human hair which could have belonged to Julie Dart. And on a curtain they found traces of diluted human blood which also matched Julie's but not mine, or that of Sams or his wife Teena. They also found tufts of mustard-coloured carpet fibre in the workshop that scientists pronounced 'indistinguishable' from tufts found on the sheet which had contained Julie's body.

At first Sams categorically denied any knowledge of Julie Dart, the murder or any kidnap attempt, but as more and more evidence came to light he changed his story a number of times. The police knew that his denials were not always to be taken seriously. He would often go away, think about what had been said, realise he could not get away with it and then come back with a new explanation, usually involving an accomplice, although he had originally said no one else was involved.

One of the most telling revelations emerged when a handwriting expert compared samples freely provided by Sams with handwritten notes sent to Leeds police after Julie's death. The notes, which discuss her murder, leave no doubt that whoever wrote them had knowledge of her death. The expert found a considerable number of similarities in the two samples and fourteen identical spelling mistakes. Although Sams initially tried to pass these off as 'coincidence', he later realised that such an explanation would never hold up in court and so he confessed he had written the notes for his mate.

By this admission Sams had linked himself with the Julie Dart murder case which, until then, he had consistently denied. It was an important turning point for the police inquiry. Another came with the discovery of the ransom money. For some time Sams maintained that his accomplice, his mate, had the money. Police had long since dismissed the existence of a mate but the missing ransom remained a loose end they needed to tie up. Answering questions about Julie, Sams inadvertently helped them do just that.

Two witnesses had come forward after the discovery of Julie's body in July to say they had seen a man with a stick on a private road close to where the body was found. The police asked Sams if that man was him but he denied it. Later, another witness claimed to have seen a red or orange coloured Metro parked not far from the spot where Julie's body was discovered. They asked if the car was his but again Sams denied it.

'I've already told you,' he insisted, 'I don't know that area at all. I've only been past there once in my life, just a few months ago when I was on my way to Stoke Summit where I was train spotting.' Going back over his statement a quick-witted officer, Detective Sergeant Tim Grogan, realised that the east coast line at Stoke Summit where Sams claimed to have been train spotting was the very same line that passed his house. He would have had no reason to go to that area to watch engines, since the very trains passed within feet of the bottom of his garden.

Sams had inadvertently provided them with a clue to the whereabouts of the cash. He had admitted being in the area close to where Julie's body was found but his reason for being there, to train spot, clearly didn't make sense. The police believed that if Sams was going to such trouble to disguise his reason for being in the area he must have a good reason for doing so. The man with a stick spotted in the area by two witnesses could have been Sams. If so, it seemed likely that the red Metro seen parked there belonged to him. It was no more than a hunch but it was to prove a good one. A search of the area with ground-probing radar equipment revealed two packages which between them contained the bulk of the ransom money paid by Shipways for my release.

By the time I was called, Lynne Dart, Julie's boyfriend Dominic and a number of other witnesses had already given evidence. I was sworn in and in response to Mr Waverley's questioning I began to explain what had happened to me from the moment I met Sams at Turnberry Road. I described the fight in the bathroom and the journey to the workshop. I recalled how he had forced me to undress and change into clothes he provided before putting me into the box for the night. I even recalled eating the hot chips but one thing was left unsaid – I did not mention the rape.

Two people in the courtroom, he and I, knew that I was not, as I had sworn, telling the 'whole truth'. Over the months I had managed to repress details of what he had done to me that night, although there were many times it would have been a relief to have had it out in the open. On one occasion I can remember asking a police woman I was chatting to about the case whether Julie Dart had been raped, in the hope it would prompt the right response, but it hadn't happened.

I don't blame the police. I lied to them about that one detail and I lied again in court, even denying under questioning that there had been any sexual contact. They were not to know that I would rather have perjured myself than stand in the witness box and try to tell that room full of strangers what he had done to me on that first night. I saw a juror brush away a tear as I described the pain and the cold of that first awful night in the box and I felt ashamed that I was not allowing these people to know exactly what sort of a bastard they were really dealing with; they didn't know the half of it but still I said nothing.

Throughout the morning I purposely kept my eyes averted from the place where I knew he would be sitting. I simply concentrated on telling my story as clearly as I could. I was clutching a lucky amethyst crystal in my fist and wearing just about every lucky charm I possessed but, as time went on, I calmed down and realised nothing bad could happen to me here. It was not until some hours later, after we returned from lunch, that I felt sufficiently relaxed to let my eyes wander around the courtroom.

There was a group of four men in the space where I had expected him to be sitting, all wearing white shirts and dark ties, obviously police. I sighed with relief. Why had nobody bothered to tell me that he wasn't even in court? I relaxed into my chair but I knew something wasn't quite right. How could he not be here, he was the one on trial. My eyes swept the four men in white shirts again, and I noticed one of them, the smallest one, sat in the middle of the others with his head bowed. He looked very small to be a policeman, I thought – but he also looked much too small to be the man who had attacked me at Turnberry Road.

Almost against my will my eyes kept returning to the little chap with thinning hair, his hands together and his head bowed. I suddenly knew it was him. That puny, shrivelled-up old man was the person who had done all this to me. Not just the eight days but the weeks and months since: the fear, the unhappiness, the sleepless nights, the paranoia. I was enraged. Although I continued to look at him throughout the rest of the time I was giving evidence, his eyes never met mine. I wanted him to look at me, I wanted to face him, stare him out, let him see that I was here watching his humiliation, but he wouldn't meet my eyes. I could see he kept snuffling as I spoke. I couldn't believe it – he was crying.

·15·

I HAD ALWAYS intended to give my evidence to the court and go home. I felt I had heard enough about what Michael Sams had done to last me a lifetime, but all that changed when I saw him. He was nothing like the man I remembered from Turnberry Road, the man who had come at me snarling with a knife in one hand and a chisel in the other. He seemed older, greyer and thinner. I shuddered at the thought of what this old man had done.

Until that point I had been worried and a little frightened. After spotting him, with his hands clasped together and head bowed, striking a pose of remorse with his snivelling, I was only angry. I don't know how I'd expected him to be. I knew the police had found him arrogant under questioning; more than one officer had spoken of his superior attitude, and I suppose I thought he would be like that in court. I couldn't believe that after what he had done to Julie Dart, a teenager with everything to live for, as well as everything he had put me through during those eight days, he was sitting in court crying. His tears could only be for the benefit of the jury. I was completely incensed and I knew I had to see the trial out.

I had to know what he was going to say and it needed to be from a ringside seat.

I sat just in front of Lynne Dart as he was called to the witness box, seventeen days after the trial began. He limped heavily – but again I suspect that was largely to engage the sympathy of the jury. I had noticed that he walked with a bit of a shuffle as I'd heard him moving about the workshop, but it was nothing like the Long John Silver type clump of the kind he was using in court.

My heart lurched as he took the oath. The man I saw in the witness box, dressed in a white shirt, dark tie and grey trousers and pullover, was a stranger to me, but the voice was one I would never forget. The defence lawyer, John Milmo QC, came straight to the point.

'Did you murder Julie Anne Dart?' he asked Sams.

'No,' came the reply.

'Did you kidnap Julie Anne Dart?'

'No.'

'Did you seek to blackmail £145,000 from Leeds City Police?'

'No.'

'Did you kidnap Stephanie Slater?'

'Yes.'

'Did you unlawfully imprison Stephanie Slater?'

'Yes.'

'Did you demand £175,000 from her employers, Shipways?'

'Yes,' he replied with a sort of choked sob.

I listened with horror to some of the details that emerged. Seemingly Sams had planned to kidnap a woman estate agent from Crewe in Cheshire, six months before he had snatched me from Turnberry Road. Forty-two-year-old Carole Jones avoided becoming a victim because as Sams waited for her outside the empty house he had arranged to view, a builder working at a neighbouring property approached him and struck up a conversation. Sams admitted that 'he couldn't get rid of him' and realised that the man would have no trouble in identifying him, so he abandoned the scheme. A week later Julie disappeared from Leeds.

Mr Milmo also questioned him about his friend, the person Sams had told the police was responsible for Julie Dart's murder. He said the friend had been storing some equipment at his workshop in Swan and Salmon Yard, Newark. He happened to call in shortly after Sams returned from the failed kidnap attempt in Crewe. Sams was feeling down because, as he said, 'I didn't have the courage, not the courage, the confidence, to go ahead. I was fed up.' He then outlined the kidnap plan to his friend, who pronounced it 'brilliant', but neither of them discussed putting it into practice.

It was an unnerving experience for me hearing Sams talk about his friend who, I had no doubt, was the 'mate' he had referred to during my captivity. The police had told me repeatedly that this man did not exist, that Sams had worked entirely alone in murdering Julie and in kidnapping me. All their evidence showed this to be the case, and while I desperately wanted to believe it, at the back of my mind there was the constant niggling doubt that they might not be right. Sams had put the fear of God into me talking about 'my mate'. Every day there had been some reference to how 'vicious' or 'nasty' he was, and I was constantly reminded how fortunate I had been in not yet having met him. 'You're lucky you didn't get him; he's a nasty piece of work, I can tell you.' I could hear it in my mind as clearly then as I had at the time it was said. Whatever the police may say, I wasn't a hundred per cent convinced that the mysterious 'mate' wasn't out there somewhere.

Sams said that around eleven o'clock on the night Julie

Dart was murdered, his friend had telephoned him at home to ask if he would drive to Skegness the following day. The friend wanted Sams to make a pornographic video of himself and a girl. I shuddered: that certainly sounded like something the mate I had heard so much about might do. Sams said he had agreed to the suggestion because he had never done anything like that before but, in the event, his friend telephoned early the following morning to cancel the arrangement, because he and the girl were still in Leeds.

Sams claimed that they were next together on Saturday 20 July watching sport on television at the workshop. At some point a news report mentioned the discovery of Julie Dart's body in a field in Lincolnshire.

'I said, "Oh, your kidnapping's gone wrong then,"' Sams told the jury. At this the friend supposedly confessed that things had gone wrong. Julie had tried to run away and he had hit her with a hammer. 'But he didn't say where or anything like that,' Sams noted.

He was later shown the letters that handwriting experts had said were written by him. He agreed that he had written them but stressed he had done so at the request of his friend. He could give no explanation as to why he went along with it, other than the fact that things were not going well in his marriage and he didn't much care what he did at that time.

The friend was also responsible for attempts to blackmail British Rail by threatening to derail an express passenger train, Sams told the court. He had considered it a 'stupid' idea.

Mr Milmo then questioned Sams about me: how had he planned and executed my kidnap, the conditions he had held me in and why he felt it necessary to do so.

It was almost convincing as he wept into his handkerchief. Almost but not quite. If he was as eaten up by remorse as he made out, why didn't he tell the truth? There couldn't have been a person in the courtroom who believed his cock and bull story about his friend. For the first time, even I believed there was no friend. The last time I had heard an explanation of that kind had been in the schoolyard: 'It wasn't me miss, it was her. I didn't do it miss, she did.'

Mr Milmo asked if Sams was prepared to name his friend but he declined to do so. 'Not at the moment, no.'

He was pathetic, even when he was speaking to the lawyer for his defence.

Michael Sams admitted that he held me handcuffed, blindfolded and gagged, with the threat of being crushed by boulders or electrocuted by the electrodes he had run through the box. An infra-red warning system which would activate a series of repeat telephone calls to his home number made the scenario, as Mr Wakerley pointed out, 'sound like something out of a James Bond film'. Much too crude for 007, however, was the large wooden board through which he had driven about two dozen nine-inch nails. If, by some miracle, I had escaped from the box and made my way towards the door, this vicious trap, laid on the floor directly in front of it, would have seriously impaired my progress through the dark workshop.

By producing this information in court Mr Wakerley threw into considerable doubt Sams' tearful claim that he had never wished me any harm. The prosecutor quoted from letters Sams sent anonymously to the press after my release. The police had started linking my kidnap with the murder of Julie Dart during the time I was being held prisoner in the workshop. Immediately I was released the newspapers began making similar links. Sams must have panicked when he read these reports because he started writing letters at once, to the police, Lynne Dart and the press, in which he admitted kidnapping me but denied any knowledge of Julie's murder. In one of these letters he recalled that after collecting the ransom he returned to me in the workshop where, hysterical, I virtually collapsed into his arms.

'Fortunately Stephanie still had on her blindfold so she was unable to see the tears streaming down my own face,' he had written. 'I am', he added, 'ashamed, upset and thoroughly disgusted at my treatment of Stephanie.' But going on to note his own suffering, he wrote about the nights since my release that he had frequently lain awake crying. He added that although he was sure I would eventually get over the trauma of it all, he never would.

However ashamed he may have been of his treatment of me Sams was not prepared to share any of the blame for Julie Dart's death. He said he personally had had no part in her murder but he knew the man who was responsible. The case for the prosecution hinged on the fact that the accomplice, his mate, did not exist and therefore it was Sams and Sams alone who was responsible for my kidnap, Julie's murder and the attempted blackmail of British Rail.

'Are we to believe there was another kidnapper?' Mr Wakerley asked. 'One who by pure coincidence used the Dove Valley Trail in South Yorkshire and the same methods for communicating messages to the police?

'The cases are so similar,' he went on, 'it was as if the criminal had left his fingerprints on them . . . The crimes for which the defendant is on trial required detailed and meticulous planning but Sams was so arrogant, so amoral that it became a game to him, a game of "catch me if you can" with the police.'

The alleged accomplice gave the prosecution endless opportunities to take Sams' story to pieces.

'When will you name your friend?' Mr Wakerley demanded.

'When I have proved that I did not kill Julie Dart. I have always said right from the beginning I would name him.'

'I'm not interested in what you said before. When will you name your friend, if he exists?'

'After the conclusion of this trial,' Sams replied without any trace of emotion.

'Next week?'

When the court had established his innocence 'as they will', Sams announced confidently, then he would name the man responsible.

The more Mr Wakerley persisted the more set the expression on Michael Sams' face became, until he was snapping answers back at the prosecutor like a petulant child.

'Forgive me Mr Sams, this is not a game. The Crown say you killed Julie Dart, you say it was your friend. Let us have his name now please.'

'Not at the moment, because I have not yet proved I didn't do it.'

The prosecutor stared intently at Sams and extended his hand towards the jury box.

'Are you involved in a game with these ladies and gentlemen?' he asked.

'No, not at all.'

'When you have proved you did not kill Julie Dart you will tell us the name of the man responsible for the death of Julie Dart?'

'I have only one chance to name that person,' replied Sams. 'It is my belief that if I had named him beforehand the police would have eliminated him. They didn't want to listen to me. They went straight on TV and said the same man had done both. The Assistant Chief Constable of West Yorkshire said he would stake his reputation that one man had done all these crimes. I said right from the start that I would prove myself innocent. I want the jury to believe me.'

Sams was clearly determined to stand his ground on the issue of naming his friend, even when the judge, Mr Justice Igor Judge, intervened:

'Mr Sams,' he said leaning towards the witness box, 'if you are not prepared to identify this man in court, the jury may find it difficult to believe he exists at all.'

Sams nodded and said that he understood that might be the case.

'Are you still not prepared to name him?' rapped out Mr Wakerley.

Again, Sams refused.

'Because you want to prove your innocence in another way?'

'Yes.'

'Then you *are* playing a game.'

'I am not playing a game Mr Wakerley, I am not.'

The prosecutor continued to question the actions of the friend who supposedly had both a key to Sams' workshop in Newark and access to his computer. The same man who, Sams had told the police, was responsible for burying the ransom money provided by Shipways.

Why was it, Mr Wakerley queried, that in the ten months between Sams' arrest and the police digging up the money at Stoke Summit, his friend had not been back to collect the cash?

'I can think of no explanation as to why that did not happen,' he answered.

'The only explanation is that he does not exist,' the prosecutor said emphatically.

'What happens to a kidnap victim when a kidnap goes wrong? Did it ever cross your mind that one of your victims might have to be killed?'

'No, it didn't, no,' Sams said looking agitated. 'I would never have been able to hurt a woman.'

'Never hurt a woman?' Mr Wakerley's eyebrows shot up into his head.

When Sams answered his voice was stilted and uneven; he sounded as if he was about to burst into tears. 'I know what you're going to say, that I hurt Stephanie Slater.'

'What are you crying for?'

'I don't know,' he replied but his body continued to shake with emotion and he pressed a handkerchief to his face to soak up the tears that by now were running freely. As I stared at him, I felt little pity. He had brought this on his own head. Having heard how he lived, in a detached house with a big garden, his own boss in his own business, it was clear he hadn't even done it for the money. I couldn't dissociate the snivelling wretch in the box from the pain and anguish he had caused. I didn't believe his tears were for real. Surely anyone capable of battering somebody to death, of keeping a human being – or indeed any living thing – blindfolded, chained and gagged in a cold dark box hour after hour, must be devoid of normal emotion. Unless of course he was crying for himself – and God knows I could understand that well enough.

Mr Wakerley seemed to regard this display of grief in much the same way I did.

'When you built that box were you crying?'

'No.'

'When you put her in that box were you crying?'

'No.'

'When you told her there were electrodes were you crying?'

'No.'

'When you manacled her ankles were you crying? When you put the gag in her mouth were you crying?'

'No. It were upsetting. It did upset me that.'

Slowly Michael Sams' credibility disintegrated. By skilful questioning, the like of which I had only ever seen before on television, Mr Wakerley exposed the man behind the façade. He had wanted to commit the perfect crime, to outwit the police and get away with it.

As the trial progressed it transpired that in 1978, while serving a nine-month prison sentence for car theft, Sams developed a tumour in his knee. By the time the tumour was diagnosed as being malignant it was too late to save the leg which was amputated above the knee. He made no secret of his resentment towards the police and the prison service, whom he considered responsible for this loss of the limb. Sams was trying to convince the jury he had been no more than an innocent pawn used, as he put it, 'as a pillock' by the cruel murderer of Julie Dart. But with each minute that passed he emerged as an ever more bitter and dangerous man: a man attempting to shift the burden of blame from himself to somebody else.

When Sams was arrested £19,000 had been discovered hidden in the workshop. Mr Wakerley addressed the jury: 'Sams told the police that on the way back from collecting the ransom his mate made clear he wanted Stephanie killed. Sams had bargained for her life, agreeing to take just £19,000 and leaving the rest to his mate in order to save Stephanie's life. Members of the jury, that was a lie.'

He wheeled around to face the defendant.

'Is the name of your friend Michael Benniman Sams? Michael Benniman Sams, the failed man?'

'No.'

'Michael Benniman Sams, the cruel man?'

'No.'

'Michael Benniman Sams, the brutal man?'

'No.'

'Michael Benniman Sams, the killer?'

The question hung in the silent courtroom.

'No.'

Describing his mate, Sams said he was about fifty years of age, five foot ten inches tall and with dark hair. He had worked for British Rail but no longer did so, he added.

Mr Wakerley asked him why, if it was the mate and not Sams who had murdered Julie Dart, her naked body had been discovered in a sheet, trussed up with rope that had both come from his workshop.

He didn't know.

'How then were traces of her blood found in your workshop?' he demanded.

'I cannot come up with an explanation.'

'The explanation is that Julie Dart was murdered in your workshop, wasn't she?'

'Not by me, definitely.'

'You wanted to be remembered as the man who got away with the money didn't you? The man who beat the police.'

'I had a good plan to kidnap Stephanie Slater,' Sams said quietly.

'Oh yes, it was a good plan, a lovely plan, a brilliant plan, but not when it ended in the death of a young woman,' Mr Wakerley accused.

'I had nothing to do with the death of Julie Dart.'

'You just can't bring yourself to admit you killed Julie Dart can you? So like a little child you have invented a friend to take the blame.'

'I had nothing to do with the death of Julie Dart, if I had I would have said so.'

Sams stuck to his story throughout, maintaining he was not prepared to name anyone until found innocent on his own account. It was a crazy implausible story but with the weight of evidence against him he probably thought it his only chance.

In his closing speech for the prosecution Mr Wakerley described Sams' story of an accomplice as 'an affront to common sense'. There was no friend: Michael Sams acted alone when he murdered Julie Dart and there were twenty separate pieces of evidence linking him to the case, the prosecutor noted.

Counsel for the defence Mr John Milmo QC said the prosecution was only guessing. Not one witness had come forward to say they had ever seen Michael Sams in the Chapeltown district of Leeds where Julie was last spotted, let alone on the night she disappeared. In addition three witnesses, previously dispatched by Wakerley as having made an understandable mistake, testified to having seen Julie on the day after she disappeared. Finally Mr Milmo asked the jury to give serious consideration to whether another man might have been involved in the crimes, as Michael Sams had repeatedly told me during my eight days in captivity.

Before sending the jury out to consider their verdict Mr Justice Judge warned them to 'think with their heads rather than react with their hearts'. Sams should not, the judge stressed, 'be convicted of one crime simply because he admitted to another.

'Michael Sams has claimed a friend kidnapped and murdered Julie Dart. Just as you may accept this evidence, you are entitled to conclude that this account of an unidentified friend who committed these crimes is untruthful. Stephanie Slater may provide positive evidence that the person who kidnapped and imprisoned her and blackmailed Shipways estate agents was responsible for the other crimes . . .

'. . . Michael Sams has said his friend was responsible for the murder of Julie Dart. If you consider that is true or may be true you will find him not guilty. If you do not believe any friend exists, then Michael Sams is solely responsible for all the crimes for which he is charged and you will find him guilty.'

It took the jury just over three hours to return their unanimous verdict. Michael Sams had gambled and lost.

I grabbed Dad's hand as the verdict was read out, and immediately I heard the word guilty I was on my feet. 'Yes!' I cried, punching the air. Behind me I could hear Lynne Dart and other members of Julie's family. They too were clearly delighted with the verdict. The judge called for order and only when the courtroom had calmed down and there was complete silence again did he turn his attention to Michael Sams.

'You are an extremely dangerous and evil man. The jury has convicted you of murder, a murder in cold blood. You deliberately strangled Julie Dart to death when your kidnapping went wrong because she had seen more than she should. Undeterred by the horror of what you had done you then turned this to your advantage by kidnapping Stephanie Slater. I have not the slightest doubt that she too was in mortal danger during the first two to three days of her captivity. If it seemed necessary to you, she, like Julie Dart, would have been murdered in cold blood.'

Referring to my kidnap and imprisonment in the wheely bin the judge quietly observed:

'However dreadful we might imagine it was, the reality must have been worse.'

I was in tears as he addressed Sams: 'Stephanie's survival was entirely due to her own remarkable courage and qualities of character which have won the admiration and respect of everyone.'

I was choked; at last everyone knew this vicious, brutal man for the cold-blooded killer he was. As Lynne Dart later said, nothing would bring Julie back but we had seen justice done, and even though Sams would not be deprived of his life he would for ever be deprived of the opportunity to harm anyone else.

Before sentencing him to four life sentences, one for Julie Dart's murder, one for each of the kidnap charges and my unlawful imprisonment, plus ten years on each blackmail charge, Mr Justice Judge described Sams as a 'callous, arrogant man who was and would for the foreseeable future remain a menace to the community'.

'There is an urgent need to protect the public from you,' he added.

'Take him down,' the judge instructed the court officers. And without a word or a trace of emotion Michael Sams was led from the witness box down the stairs to the cells. At fifty-one years of age he would never again be free.

Three days later Sams called police officers to his cell and admitted to the murder of Julie Dart on the 10th of July, the day after her disappearance. During her captivity she was never blindfolded because she had already seen Sams when he picked her up in Chapeltown. In any case, it didn't matter: he had always intended that she should die.

·16·

SAMS' CONFESSION AND his admission that there was not and never had been a mate should have closed the book for me. For months I had felt that with the court case behind me I would be able pick up the pieces and get on with my life. I knew things wouldn't be quite the same as before but I was determined to give it my best shot.

I had already decided that although the people of Birmingham had been wonderful, with their letters and messages of support, I would have to leave the city if I was to make any sort of fresh start. The minute I left the house I felt as if I was on display: people seemed to be pointing me out in the street. Perhaps it was my own paranoia, but that's how it felt.

I had spoken to Stacey about going to live on the Isle of Wight. Shortly before the trial began we had spent a few days' holiday there and Stacey was almost as smitten with the island as I was. A crazy, funny, smart and incredibly understanding person, Stacey had seen me through the worst of times. I had told her everything about my eight days in captivity and she, more than anyone else, knew the fears and roller-coaster emotions I had experienced since my release. When I wanted to talk she would listen, and if I didn't she would never ask questions; she has been an enormous source of emotional support. Mostly we would stay at my house and watch television – or just talk. She shares my love of animals, tall blond men and the ridiculous, and has the ability almost always to help me see the funny side of a situation. We rarely went out, but on one of the few occasions that we did, a group of young lads, clearly with too much drink inside them, recognised me and began making cracks.

'Hiya Steph, wanna look at a house with me?'

'Lend us a fiver Steph, you must be worth a few quid now.'

I was almost used to this kind of thing but felt like leaving. Stacey was furious and went over to the group to sort them out. Just the sight of her, all five foot three inches with a shock of red hair on top, squaring up to this gang of six-foot drunken Brummies was enough to make me smile. She did get rid of them too.

When we first discussed moving to the island it seemed like an impossible dream. I was still frightened to be on my own. Even if I went into a shop by myself I had to park my car right outside the door: I thought of it as my emergency escape route, and if I couldn't see it I was frantic. I would never pass the Shipways office if I could help it, frequently going miles out of my way to avoid driving past the window. I knew I would not be able to cope with living on my own, even in the Isle of Wight. But I also knew that Stacey had responsibilities in Birmingham: she lived with her widowed Mum and had a full-time job working with people she liked.

We made tentative plans and talked about an unspecified date 'before Christmas'.

Meanwhile, I had convinced myself that in order to tackle my future head on as I wanted to, I first had to lay a ghost from the past. The trial was over, Michael Sams was in prison for the rest of his life and I knew for sure there was no mate. I no longer had to keep looking over my shoulder. In theory I should have nothing to fear. I had been back to Turnberry Road with the press and relived much of the horror of the kidnap experience in Nottingham Crown Court. However, it seemed to me there was one essential piece of the jigsaw I had not yet attempted to deal with: the workshop. I had spent eight days of my life, the worst period of my twenty-five years up to the kidnap date, in a place I had never even seen because of the blindfold. I became increasingly convinced that it was necessary to return there.

Since the moment I'd entered my own front door on the night of my release I had a strange feeling of not being a hundred per cent in touch, not a real part of what was going on. I was a changed and different person to the one Michael Sams had taken from Turnberry Road and I was trying to deal with that. But at the same time I felt I had not managed to get a real grip on exactly what had happened in Newark.

The whole idea of being kidnapped and kept in a bin, taken out and fed, allowed to go to the loo, put back and locked up until he chose to let me out, now seemed unreal. I wanted to face 'the thing' head on but an essential part of it kept slipping from my grasp like soap in a bath tub. Occasionally I would think I had it crystal clear in my mind. What had happened to me was bizarre, macabre, the stuff that horror stories are made of, but the clarity existed only for a moment, then it would be gone, swamped beneath a landslide of 'sensible thoughts' that urged me to put it out of my mind. After all, I was alive, wasn't I? I had survived. I heard Mr Wakerley tell the court that it was my compliance, my determination to build a rapport with Sams that had saved my life. It had worked. I was here. I was a hero, for Christ's sake, according to all the newspapers. So what was my problem?

Over the course of the year and a half between my release and the trial a number of the press assigned to the case became people I still regard as friends. I had signed contracts with the *Sun* and with Central Television, my local TV station. From time to time I would talk to Andrew Parker from the *Sun* and had come to regard him as a mate. Keith Wilkinson from Central Television was a local Birmingham journalist who had been at the press conference held just after my release. What started off as a professional relationship turned into a friendship I continue to value.

It was to Keith that I first expressed my desire to return to the workshop. He thought I was mad. He wasn't the only one: most of the people I discussed it with could see no virtue in going back. Yet I knew it was the right thing to do. As far as I could see there was only one of two ways it could go. Either I would walk into the place and the enormity of what had gone on would hit me right between the eyes – I would recapture the horror of my time there and then leave, devastated but ready to begin the process of rebuilding my sanity – or I would go back and experience nothing.

In the event it was neither of these. Keith Wilkinson arranged the visit. Those now in charge of the workshop rented to Michael Sams had not been slow to capitalise on its potential following Sams' arrest and were now charging a fee to anyone who wanted to view the building. They were not short of takers.

Central Television agreed to pay the fee in exchange for some film footage. It was a dismal day when we left Birmingham but it cleared as we got further north. My

Dad was in the car with me and as he and Keith talked together about the places we were passing I looked out of the window. It seemed strange to think I had travelled this route before but unable to see any of the countryside we were now passing. Lying in the front seat of Sams' car, bound, blindfolded and gagged, I had been terrified. Even the sound of other traffic on the road had been frightening, but it seemed quite different in daylight and without any restrictions.

During my eight days in captivity I was convinced I was being held miles from anywhere. Sams had nurtured the belief when we arrived at the workshop, telling me not to scream and then adding 'not that anyone would hear you out here'. During the day the radio was always on but, for the most part, the nights were quiet. Only occasionally did I hear the sound of a passing car or train and I felt that that was probably more to do with wind direction than distance. Wind was something I heard plenty of: it seemed to whistle around the outside of the building all night. I seriously began to consider the idea that I was up on the moors somewhere.

It was an enormous shock to approach the Swan and Salmon Yard I had heard referred to so often in court, the place in which I had spent so many hours of painful isolation. I now realise it was only a couple of hundred yards from a main road. A river overhung by mature trees ran behind it and on a hill beyond that stood the ruins of the most magnificent old castle. It was a very beautiful location. I was astonished to think that so much life had been going on so close to where I had lain alone and terrified. I had thought of Bob, as I then knew him, driving home through streets with shops lit up and people walking in them when he left me in the evening, but it had never occurred to me that those shops and people were just around the first corner.

The workshop building was hundreds of years old, Keith had discovered. As we turned off the main road and drove the thirty yards or so to the workshop I saw the entrance was through a stone archway, just wide enough to park a car. This was how he had managed to shuffle me into and out of the building so quickly and efficiently. The large metal door I had seen in my mind's eye was in fact wooden; only the runners it opened and closed on were made of metal, which had made the grating sound I grew so familiar with.

My Dad clasped my hand as we entered the cold, damp building: neither one of us knew what to expect. Beneath my feet the concrete which gave way to cobbled stone felt strangely familiar, but nothing else did. It was smaller, much smaller, than I had thought it was. The police had torn the place to pieces in their search for forensic evidence and whereas the place they had first entered to arrest Sams had been cramped and cluttered, the building was now virtually stripped. Above me I could see the old wooden beam I had spotted on one occasion when I had managed to force my head against the lid of the plastic wheely bin until it opened just a fraction of an inch. Even the ceiling was lower than I expected.

I was chatting to my Dad and Keith but I was also trying to take in every detail of my surroundings at the same time. There was the old telephone I had so desperately listened for on my last night when Bob was out collecting the ransom from Kevin Watts. So, I worked out, the microwave must have been on that shelf and the radio up there next to it. By turning this way and that and trying to recall exactly which direction certain noises came from, the radio, the ping of the microwave, the grating of the door, I could work out where other things must have been. The bin over there in the corner, the chair closer to the radio, the bucket toilet, the mattress: I could fit them all into place.

On the floor were the battered remains of an electric fire. I wondered if this had been the one Bob switched on in the morning as I sat eating porridge and sipping tea. I remembered how I had felt as the warmth penetrated my cold and aching bones after a night in the bin and I reached down to touch the broken metal carcass, but it was just an old electric fire, not a talisman with magical properties.

I had hoped for a breakthrough of some kind, an opportunity to reel around clutching my head and shouting, 'Oh my God, this is it. Jesus, this is where it happened. Yes, yes, this is the place where I was destroyed.' I felt I needed something to make me feel more in touch with the events of those eight days between the kidnap and my release, some gigantic hurdle to overcome before I could tackle the future. I wasn't the person I had been before it happened and I think I felt that if I could do something sufficiently frightening or momentous I could jerk myself back into being that person, drop back into my place in life, become a round peg in a round hole again.

The workshop didn't provide any of the answers I was looking for. It was a spooky experience in one way but in another way I felt like nothing more than an interested bystander. I knew I was in the place where I had experienced the worst moments of my life, where I had been raped, kept continually blindfolded, at best in conditions that were uncomfortable, at worst in pain, but it no longer seemed part of what was going on for me. I guess I felt like people do when, after the operation, they see their own tonsils floating in a jar. Interesting but not worth two hundred and fifty quid.

One by one I was crossing off the possibilities. I had felt sure the trial would provide the turning point I sought but it didn't. I had then pinned a lot of hope on my visit to the workshop providing a catalyst but that hadn't worked either. Eventually, I had to face the fact that there wasn't going to be a miracle that would transport me back in time and allow me to re-occupy the life I had lived before the kidnap. I couldn't pretend that the things that had happened to me had not. I couldn't kid myself any longer that those same things wouldn't have a lasting effect on my life because I knew they would and already did. Even though I was back at home, living with Mum and Dad in familiar surroundings, it was as if there were two Stephanie Slaters: the one I had been before the kidnap and the one I was now.

I had never been claustrophobic but now I felt uncomfortable in any confined space. Not just the obvious places like lifts or shops, but even being in a shower cubicle made me anxious. I couldn't bear to be left in the house alone but I couldn't stand leaving the house to be stared at in the street. From being a clean person, I had become almost obsessively fastidious: only an hour after having a bath I would be back in the bathroom scrubbing away at myself, a routine with which I drove everyone mad five or six and often many more times a day. I knew things couldn't go on as they were.

For years I had planned, eventually, to live on the Isle of Wight. As a child I had always hated leaving the island when annual holidays came to an end but although I had been sad to leave after the few days that Stacey and I had spent there just before the trial, I had promised myself that when I returned next time it would be to live. After weeks of deliberation Stacey and I packed up our cars, and complete with carrier bags and a pair of canaries, we left Birmingham behind in October 1993.

Shortly before leaving home I had received a letter from

a writer who was planning a book on Michael Sams. He wanted to have a chat with me about what had happened during the eight days in the workshop. I stood in the sitting room rereading his letter and I shook with fear and rage. It seemed incredible that the whole sorry saga was continuing. Sams was in prison, Julie Dart was dead and I was, I hoped, about to make a new start but still it wouldn't go away. I wasn't annoyed with the writer: his was a job like any other, and at least he was giving me an opportunity to tell my side of the story, but there had already been a number of true crime paperbacks on the event. I hadn't read any of them, it would have been too painful to do so. 'The girl in the box' might be a great headline but nobody else could begin to know how it was for me during that time.

Keith Wilkinson, my journalist friend from Central Television, had urged me to write a book of my own and although I had given the idea a lot of serious thought, there was a part of me that believed it was time to leave the whole thing alone and let the fuss die down. Now, however, it started to look as if public interest would never go away.

I was worried by the prospect of the Michael Sams story becoming public knowledge. He had already made veiled references to the police about 'a secret' we shared. I had kept my promise by continuing to deny there had been any sexual contact, up to and during the trial, not through any sense of misplaced loyalty but because of fear, but he didn't have anything to worry about any more. In prison, serving four life sentences, Michael Sams would never be free again – what did he have to lose? I decided that if there was to be a book about the girl in the box it should be written by the one person still alive, who had been there.

I didn't want to write about the rape and before work

on this book began, I tried every way I could think of to persuade myself it wasn't relevant to the story. In many ways, it was realising how hard I worked at persuading myself it didn't matter to the book, that made me see how keenly I had worked to make it irrelevant to my life. I wanted to brush it under the carpet and forget it ever happened. I told myself that my parents had suffered enough. I knew it was a source of comfort to my Mum that 'at least he didn't touch you'; she had said so often enough. I told myself that people might not understand. I had admitted trying to build up a relationship with Sams, talking to him, sharing a joke, even hugging him. There would always, I reasoned, be somebody willing to take it a step further, to believe that I offered sex in exchange for my life. And God knows what Sams would say if allowed free rein. The court had already heard of sad sexual fantasies involving a woman called 'Julie D' written on his computer before he was arrested.

I could give myself any number of reasons why I hadn't spoken up about the rape then and why I didn't want to now. There was an element of truth in all of them. I had been horrified by the rape but when it happened it seemed in one way an extension of the violence he had already shown towards me. In court the defence barrister, Mr Milmo QC, tried to imply that Sams was not a violent man. I strongly disagreed. Even though he later displayed acts of kindness such as bathing my feet, I felt the whole relationship between us was based on violence. For eight days I lived with the permanent threat of death hanging over me. Only when I reached my own front door on the night of my release, did I feel sure I was not going to be killed. I tried to suppress the feeling all the time – if I hadn't I would have been too terrified to speak to him. I knew only too well how dispensable I was.

He had fought with me and hurt me in the bathroom

at Turnberry Road; he had snarled and struggled and would, I believe, have killed me there and then, if he'd had to. With a false leg he was too slow to make a getaway if things went wrong. His contingency plan must have been murder. He blindfolded, bound and gagged me before driving me away, against my will, to where he held me in appalling conditions until he decided he would let me go. How could I be surprised when he raped me? He proved every time he forced me back into the box that I was his to do exactly what he liked with.

The truth is that I was ashamed of what had happened. On the night of my release I didn't want to go through the intimate examination I knew would be necessary. I hadn't had a bath or a shower for eight days, I knew I smelled and constantly apologised for it to the police doctor who took samples from my skin, hair and beneath my nails. I didn't want to discuss the details of exactly what had happened with anyone, let alone complete strangers and certainly not in a courtroom. I simply couldn't have done it. I didn't want Mum or Dad to be forced to put up with any more. We have never been a family that discussed sex openly and the thought of dropping the word 'rape' into a conversation being held in the sanctity of Mum's sitting room was unthinkable. And, in addition to all the other good and worthy reasons was the fact that even before he was arrested and I had an opportunity to study his photograph, I remembered the grubby little man I had met up with outside Turnberry Road and I didn't want anyone to know he had been anywhere near me.

After my release when talking to the police or to the press I always tried to tell the absolute truth about what had happened except if asked directly about sexual contact with Sams; then I would lie and say there had been none. It was simply a section of the chain of events I omitted from my story. I know now it was wrong to do it but at the time it didn't feel as if I had a choice and, like so many lies, once told it was almost impossible to retract. Many, many times I would have liked to have got it off my chest, particularly before Sams' case came to trial, but I didn't.

I had searched for months for the hidden doorway to my future. I imagined that when I opened it and walked through I would leave the past behind me and live happily ever after on the 'other side'. I realise now what a crazy, simplistic idea that was. I always thought I had to confront what had happened to me and get over it. I now know it's a matter of confronting it and living with it.

After our move to the Isle of Wight in October and beginning to work on this book things became clearer. Not in the dramatic way I had expected; there was just a slow but gradual understanding that I couldn't change what had happened in the past, but that I did have some say in the future. At Christmas I went home to Mum and Dad and told them the full story. I had imagined I would sit them down together and explain as gently as I could that as well as having been kidnapped I had been raped, that it hadn't been my fault and that I was now prepared to deal with it. Of course it didn't happen like that. We didn't sit down and hold hands and cry together in the way these things happen in films. Mum and I had a row. I blurted it out while we were upstairs, she went downstairs and blurted it out to Dad. But at least it was out in the open and we were able to talk, albeit in a stilted, jagged way. I think I knew deep down that they might always have known without realising it, in that uncanny way parents have.

A huge step forward came when I successfully applied for a job at Carisbrooke Castle, one of my favourite places on the island. The job involved being a representative for English Heritage during the summer season, and although

I was very nervous about it and wrote several letters of resignation before my first day, it was an important breakthrough for me. It gave my life a focus, but much more importantly, it put me in a situation where I was seeking out members of the public to talk to, rather than skulking around waiting to be pointed out.

There have been numerous incidents on the island where I have been recognised, but never any unpleasantness. For the most part, people were wonderfully kind and supportive. Sometimes I spoke with tourists at the castle not knowing they were aware of who I was, until at the end of our conversation they might wink or touch my arm and say 'Good luck Stephanie'. Nobody could take offence at that. Little by little I realised my paranoia was diminishing. I made friends with my work colleagues, I went to the local pub with Stacey and made friends with the landlord and locals. I began picking up the threads of my life.

I no longer expect to return to the person I once was: I know that there will always be some residue of my experience in my life. I still have the scar on my palm where Sams' knife cut into me in the bathroom at Turnberry Road but I now think of it as *my* scar, not the scar caused by *his* knife. I am still obsessional about personal hygiene, but I no longer think about why I am doing it, and one day perhaps the need to do it will disappear. I still have good days and bad days but, I'm happy to say, the former outweigh the latter.

Since deciding to bring the rape into the open I have felt free to talk to a counsellor who has helped me a lot in coming to terms with what happened. For a long time after the event I wondered why it had happened to me; whether there was something about me that made Sams think it was all right to kidnap and rape me. I even wondered if in some way it might have been my fault. I now know that I was just part of a sick plot hatched by a sick mind.

I feel no sympathy for Michael Sams. I am glad he is in prison, and for what he did to me and to Julie Dart I hope he stays there for the rest of his life.

I'm still taking each day as it comes, but optimistically. The job at Carisbrooke Castle ended with the close of the tourist season, but hopefully next year will offer new opportunities. Stacey is keen to start up her own business in the near future and reckons she might be able to find work for an extra pair of hands. I fully intend to remain on the island. Even the threat that Michael Sams may eventually be moved to one of the high-security prisons here would not be sufficient to drive me away. I wouldn't like it but I wouldn't leave.

I want to be stronger than I am at the moment, and I am determined to achieve that. A few months ago Stacey left the island to spend a week's holiday with her Mum in Birmingham. I told her I would be perfectly okay on my own. I made no arrangements to visit anyone or to go out, and I didn't have a drop of alcohol in the house. The first night was hell. I continually saw things out of the corner of my eye, heard noises, checked windows. I paced up and down for hours and vowed I would never be alone again. The second night was better.

There is still a long way to go but at least I feel I am on the road now, and I will eventually get to where I want to be. For months I locked myself away. I didn't feel like the heroine the papers were talking about, I didn't feel brave at all. I just felt lucky to be alive.

After Michael Sams' trial Julie Dart's grandmother, a lovely grey-haired lady, took me to one side. 'Our Julie's gone,' she told me, 'but you have your whole life in front of you; go out and enjoy it. He kept you prisoner for eight days, love, don't give him the rest of your life.'

And I won't.